How To Write Book Reports

Analyzing and Evaluating Fiction, Drama, Poetry and Non-Fiction

by

Walter James Miller

Professor of English
New York University

and

Elizabeth Morse-Cluley

Director of Publications
Mercy College
Lecturer, New York University

AN ARCO BOOK
Published by Prentice Hall Press
New York, NY 10023

An Arco Book
Published by Prentice Hall Press
A Division of Simon & Schuster, Inc.
Gulf + Western Building
One Gulf + Western Plaza
New York, NY 10023

PRENTICE HALL PRESS is a trademark of Simon & Schuster, Inc.

Manufactured in the United States of America

3   4   5   6   7   8   9   10

Library of Congress Cataloging in Publication Data

Miller, Walter James, 1918–
   How to write book reports.

   Summary: A guide to reading and writing critically,
to produce a book report.
   1. Report writing.   2. English language—Composition
and exercises.   3. Criticism. [1. Report writing.
2. English language—Composition and exercises.
3. Criticism] I. Morse-Cluley, Elizabeth. II. Title.
LB2369.M46   1984   808'.02   84-6159
ISBN 0-668-05909-5 (pbk).

CONTENTS

Chapter 1

The Purpose and Practice of Book Report Writing

THE PURPOSE AND PRACTICE OF BOOK REPORT WRITING

Why?
Why write a book report?
What possible value could it have for me?
What relationship to my life?

Did such questions bug you when you first got the assignment? Or did they hit you only after you got bogged down somewhere in the work?

No matter. Those are smart questions, real questions, and you deserve answers. These answers should lead us well into the more practical problem:

How do I write a book report?

The Report Situation

The word of permanent, lifetime value here is *report*. No matter how little or how much you have to do with books after you leave school, you will always have to give *reports*.

Your golf club or your civic association will ask you to report on their membership drive. Your boss will send you to Alaska to find out why your company's trucks are not doing so well there. He will want a preliminary report, progress reports, and a final report.

Throughout your life, you will find that every assignment you get will require a report or a series of reports. A reporter is literally one who (*-er*) carries (*-port-*) back (*re-*) something he or she was sent out to get: something needed—*some answers to some questions*—something valuable to people who will read or hear the report.

But before your report becomes valuable to others, it's valuable to you, and for many reasons. First of all, the very fact that, throughout the work, you are aiming to *do a report on it* influences the way you do the work. You have been given some questions to answer, and they outline for you not only the way you must finally compose the report, but they actually guide you in doing the investigation. *Being in a report situation gives you focus and direction.*

Then, when you submit the report, you are offering your proof that you have completed the work. In the "real world," it's axiomatic: You haven't finished a job until you've signed the report. That signature, on a report that goes into the permanent records, is your proof of your competence, your mastery of a situation, and your integrity. So after a while you take pride in organizing and composing a report with style, finesse, and with a flourish.

Writing reports in school, then, is not just your way of proving that you did the lab work, completed the library research, or analyzed a book. It is also genuine preparation for actual professional and social life. Rather than see a book report as artificial, academic busy-work, it's better to face the larger picture. Unless you learn how to handle the lab report, the research paper, and the simplest of these—the book report—you might never learn how to report well on the club's membership drive or on the failure of a fleet of trucks in Alaskan climate.

The Book Report Situation

Just like any adult report situation, the student book report situation poses very definite questions. You must provide accurate, satisfactory, stimulating answers to questions such as these:

1. What is the book about? What does the author have to say on his subject? What seem to be his conclusions?

2. What approaches and techniques does he use to reach, interest, involve, and convince the reader?

3. What is my personal judgment of the value of (1) his content and (2) his style?

Now notice that judgment (3) is *your discovery*. It's your own original contribution. *Your excitement in doing a report—any report—will mount as you get closer to exercising your hard-earned right to make that judgment, experience that discovery* (3). And you earn that right by proving that you have conscientiously studied and evaluated the materials and problems involved (1,2). Experienced report writers will tell you that it's precisely this excitement in reaching and expressing a responsible judgment that gives them the energy, the drive to write the report.

Your Basic Assumptions

When you analyze and evaluate any book, you are on firm ground, you know exactly what you're looking for, if you keep in mind these basic assumptions about the nature, purpose, and value of all literature.

Literature provides us with much needed vicarious experience. Vicarious experience is needed for at least three reasons. Any writing may appeal to us for one, two, or all three of these reasons.

1. We need to *extend* our experience. We are confined to one period in history, to one place at a time, often to one set of circumstances. You cannot be present in fifth century Britain, but you can experience it vicariously by reading Joy Chant's *The High Kings*. You cannot nor would you want to live in a Soviet prison today. But you do need to know about such circumstances. And you can get closer to them, and safely so, by reading Lev Kopelev's *Ease My Sorrows*. You might not yet have experienced a Grand Passion, or made a great discovery, but you do want at least to know about such human adventures, distant as they

now are to you as Camelot and *sharaska*. And so you read Emily Brontë's *Wuthering Heights* or James D. Watson's *The Double Helix*.

2. We always feel a deep urge to *intensify* even that experience we have already gained firsthand. We have all been to school; we all once had to learn how to get along with our classmates. So why do we read, with great interest, F. Scott Fitzgerald's "The Freshest Boy," which takes up this very common, everyday problem? Precisely because we are always hungry for fresh insight into old and ordinary experiences.

Very often, we can *intensify* our understanding of a past experience only by *extending* our knowledge of it. And so, years after our national agonies over Southeast Asia, we desperately read Colonel Archimedes L.A. Patti's *Why Vietnam?*. We are shocked to discover that there were many vital facts withheld from us before and during that war, facts that now make us understand it better. These revelations, characteristic of so much writing, illustrate the third main function of literature.

3. We need to extend and intensify our experience so as to conduct our own affairs with greater poise and wisdom in the future. From a nonfiction work like *Why Vietnam?* we can learn how to proceed with greater caution lest we plunge with pathetic ignorance into yet another blind situation. From fiction like *Wuthering Heights* we may become aware of the danger of ignoring the demands of the Grand Passion.

Good literature, then, provides us with vicarious adventures which supplement our own limited experiences, gives us insight into our past and present circumstances, and gives us greater confidence and curiosity as we face the future. Literature makes us want to live more fully.

Vicarious Experience

You know better what you're doing, as you evaluate a book, if you understand how these vicarious adventures manage to meet these needs. Let us take a closer look at the five works already mentioned—two works of nonfiction, a short story, a collection of tales, and a novel.

★ In *Ease My Sorrows*, Lev Kopelev begins a long prison term because, while he was an officer in the Soviet army, he stood up for the human rights of German civilians.

★ In *Why Vietnam?*, Colonel Patti tells us about his personal experiences with the Vietnamese rebels: They wanted their freedom from their French rulers and modeled their Declaration of Independence on the classic American document, but America turned her back and instead helped the French return to power.

★ In "The Freshest Boy," Basil Lee looks forward to his first year at St. Regis where he expects to excel in sports, scholarship, and social life. But Lewis Crum reminds Basil that back in their hometown school, he had succeeded only in being unpopular.

★ In *Wuthering Heights*, wild and passionate Catherine agrees to marry a rich, refined neighbor even though she still loves Heathcliff, a penniless, untutored orphan.

★ In *The High Kings,* a queen hears that her husband will divorce her and marry another.

Why do we go on reading? In each case, the author invites us to be involved in other people's predicaments. But *are* they "other people's"? Haven't we all faced somewhat similar problems, and don't they all have one common denominator?

How to survive in a new situation. How to realize our fondest hopes in the face of hostile reality. How to break old habits that defeat us. How to know—and assert—our rights in difficult circumstances. Whether—and how—to give up one benefit in order to gain another.

In short, we have all, at one time or another, been *thrown off balance*. All writers, regardless of their subject or their medium, must invoke our sympathy by plunging us into this common human predicament: *disequilibrium*. Authors must involve us in the human struggle to reach, no matter how gropingly, a new balance, a new certainty.

But while literature involves us in problems basically akin to our own, it does so with a crucial difference. In real life, we can be so deeply immersed in a situation we can't get above it long enough to see its shape and direction, to see it and to know it for its real worth. We may be carried away, blinded by emotion or by half-knowledge. We tend to lose our perspective, our sense of proportion, our objectivity.

In literature, though, no matter how much we seem to become involved, we experience the struggle only vicariously. We sympathize, even identify with Kopelev, Basil, or Catherine as they grope and err, but we still keep a part of ourselves separate, aloof, critical of their behavior. We can be both inside and outside their lives. For we ourselves are not taking the real risks. The characters, so to speak, are suffering on our behalf.

Free to observe their predicaments with some detachment, we gain perspective on them, a calm perspective often denied us in real life. We begin to sense patterns of cause and effect, patterns of meaning in their circumstances—and hence in our own. The author's characters may triumph over or be overwhelmed by life's questions, but either way, we readers survive and we have the answers, the full benefit of "other people's" experiences.

Some Basic Criteria

So, you are already equipped with some basic expectations, some simple standards by which to judge any book you have to report on. You can ask yourself:

★ Has the author created a climate in which I can be involved emotionally and intellectually?

★ Has the author extended, intensified, or accelerated my experience?

★ Has he or she helped me gain a sense of transcendency over life?

Three Possible Approaches

You will be greatly relieved, and far better prepared to write your book reports, if you realize you have a choice of several different approaches and emphases. You may naturally adopt the ones that best suit your own experience and interests at the time of writing. In other words, you will vary your approach and emphasis as time goes on.

The Naive Approach

The easiest approach is simply to tell how the book impresses a naive layperson—you! You offer your personal, modest, nonspecialist's reactions for what they are worth. You make no pretensions to any specialized knowledge or *authoritative* judgment.

And your reactions are worth far more than you suppose. We are always interested in discovering the impact a work has on a newcomer to the field. Exploit the role of that newcomer! Your teachers, for example, need your candid reactions to guide them in planning future assignments and class discussions. And for you, this is excellent practice in writing—to be describing an experience for what it is, a series of fresh discoveries, puzzlements, delights, or disappointments. Such writing helps you to develop a spontaneous style.

The Authoritative Approach

But even you, a naive layperson most of the time, will sometimes find yourself in a position to be authoritative in your attitude. Let us suppose your father, a surfcaster, has for many years been teaching you how to fish from the beach for flounder, bass, bluefish, and croaker. You pick up Joseph J. Cook and William L. Wisner's *Coastal Fishing for Beginners*. You are no naive layperson now. You are a serious critic. You are really able to answer for us: *Is* this a good book for beginners? And *why*? What would you have added or changed? The very knowledge now that you are making a responsible judgment will make you proceed more deliberately and give you a different kind of satisfaction from what you enjoyed in your "naive" book report on a Greek play.

In this case, you are able to function as an authoritative report writer because you are able to tell us whether the book has the right contents and approach for the job it undertakes. What other responsibilities are authoritative critics expected to take on? They should be able to:

★ place a new book in the history of its type

★ compare it with other major works on the subject

★ identify the author's influences, his sources, the "school" or "trend" he belongs to

★ judge his originality

★ compare this new book with the author's other works and sum up his contributions to date

★ employ a somewhat specialized vocabulary to describe and evaluate the new book's structure and style

★ venture a prediction as to the effect the book will have on readers, other writers, the course of literature

In other words, the authoritative critic assumes responsibility for placing an individual work in whatever larger cultural context is relevant.

Clearly, at this stage of the game, you will not be able to use the authoritative approach very often. Fortunately, you have two alternatives—the naive approach and what we call the "two-track" approach.

The "Two-Track" Approach

Even now, and increasingly so as you write more and more book reports, you will be able to *combine* the naive and the authoritative approaches. In those areas where you can react only as a nonspecialist, you will write from that point of view. Whenever you come to an area where you can speak with some authority, you will.

For example, suppose you have been assigned to do a report on Voltaire's *Candide*. For the most part, you may use a naive approach because you can't speak authoritatively about Voltaire's world. As a naif, you are learning about this world from him. But, it just so happens that you have also read Voltaire's *Zadig*. Here is a subject on which you can be somewhat of an authority: how the two books compare in subject matter, style, and conclusions. You *can* place *Candide* in a larger context.

And so as you gain more and more experience in reporting on books, you will acquire more and more specialized knowledge which will make it increasingly likely that you will be writing "two-track" reports. In this book, for example, you have already learned *generally* what to *demand* of a book.

You will be able to show in your book reports that you have higher—or at least more definite—standards now. And as we go on, you will even pick up some of that specialized critical terminology and historical knowledge which characterize the authoritative approach.

But a word of caution: To write well and interestingly, let the personal impression, not the authoritative observation, set the tone for your report.

Five Possible Emphases

In your class discussions, you are already aware that different teachers emphasize different aspects of literature. Indeed, the same teacher may emphasize a different aspect in each work studied. The reasons are obvious, practical, and very human. You can't cover everything, you have to start someplace, and you do have your own preferences. So, teacher or student, critic or common reader, you tend to favor—or at least to begin with—one of several typical emphases. It helps to know what the possibilities are.

The Ideological Emphasis

The oldest—and still in some respects the most primitive—criterion for judging art is the moral criterion. Many critics throughout history have agreed with the ancient Greek philosopher Plato that a work should be judged first in terms of the moral effect it might have on its audience. Plato's contemporaries, the leaders of the Spartan state, went so far as to censor even Homer, allowing young people to hear only those passages of *The Iliad* and *The Odyssey* that might help build Spartan character. The French neoclassicist playwright Jean Racine felt that emotions should not be expressed on the stage except to show the chaos they cause! And after the romanticist Brontë's novel *Wuthering Heights* appeared, some critics wondered whether it was "advisable to create beings like Heathcliff."

In other words, the so-called moral emphasis is on the content, the subject matter, the message (theme and tone) of the work. Here you discuss mainly *what* the author says rather than *how* he says it, and you tend to judge his writing according to the view of life that it fosters. In effect, you enter into an argument with an author about whether he is *right*.

Obviously, at one extreme, and in certain societies, the moral approach has dangerous implications for the writer's right to write and the reader's right to read. But at the other end of the spectrum, in a free society, this emphasis has its intellectual value. There is nothing wrong with speculating on the effect a book can have on certain audiences so long as guidance rather than censorship is intended. And, again in a free society, it is understood that every author *does* offer his work for criticism, including criticism for his ideology.

In reporting on John Milton's poetic drama *Samson Agonistes*, for example, you might justifiably take offense at his assumption that, for their own good, women must be controlled by men. Just as Milton had the right to explore the idea, so you have the right to reject it and warn readers that it's there.

In writing a report on James Joyce's *Finnegans Wake*, you might consider whether he is right in assuming that a sleeping person sinks into the "collective unconscious" of the human race — or whether such a thing even exists. In reporting on Maxwell Anderson's verse drama *Winterset*, you might wonder whether he is justified in his interpretation of the Sacco-Vanzetti case.

The Aesthetic Emphasis

Rather than stress *what*, you could stress *how* an author writes, discussing mainly his/her artistic maneuvers and innovations, and their aesthetic success. Thus, in reporting on *Finnegans Wake*, you might emphasize *how* Joyce represents the "collective unconscious," and whether his portrayal of our dream life is convincing and successful. In reporting on Anderson's *Winterset*, you might explore the question of whether the verse forms he chooses to use are suitable for twentieth-century speech. Wondering what to emphasize in your report on Brontë's *Wuthering Heights*, you might be most excited by the technique of narration that she uses: having a servant recount the lives of Catherine and Heathcliff to a visitor in the area who in turn recounts them to us. What is the psychological effect of this technique on the reader? What does the technique tell us about our knowledge of human affairs?

For you as a student of writing, an author's literary *style* may be the most exciting aspect for you to stress. In a book report on *Look Homeward, Angel*, you may be fascinated by Thomas Wolfe's sentence rhythms, variations of sentence length and sentence patterns, and use of figures of speech and symbols. What makes this author's style unique and effective?

The Sociological Emphasis

When you read Upton Sinclair's *The Jungle*, you might well find that your main reaction is indignation at the social injustices Sinclair exposes. You have vicariously experienced the risks and agonies that immigrant workers were subjected to around 1900. Very likely, to be true to your own reactions, you will stress these revelations in writing your book report.

In so doing, you will be following a growing tendency in the past century or so to see the arts in their social context. This emphasis was formalized for us by the French author Emile Zola who, in both his theoretical writing and his novels, tried to be outright Darwinist, that is, to study his characters mainly as products of their heredity and their environment.

Zola believed that to accomplish this an author had to provide massive documentation about the society in which the characters live. One net result in modern fiction and drama is that people are seen less as enjoying free will and more as living lives strongly determined by outer circumstances, especially the class in which they are born.

For example, a pre-Zolaist writer could have his virtuous characters rising above any adverse circumstances, simply because "virtue triumphs." But post-Zolaist writers often show virtue defeated in a world governed not by a moral system but by greed and vested interests. Thus, in *The Jungle*, many honest, hardworking people are exploited and destroyed. Only one, Jurgis Rudkus, escapes, and only because of a coincidence. He happens to wander into a Socialist meeting and what he hears gives him hope and energy.

If you have a sociological interest, this approach to a book should give you a field day. In reporting on *The Jungle*, for example, you might agree with Sinclair that the evils he exposes should be corrected wherever they exist (to some extent they still do), but disagree with his ending and his conclusions.

In reporting on Jane Austen's *Pride and Prejudice*, you might be astonished to note that we rarely get any idea of how the characters make their living. Careful checking will reveal to you that the author pays little attention to the fact that the English gentry and aristocracy *don't* make a living. They live off the work of servants and farmers who are assiduously ignored by characters and author. You might decide to write about this "invisible" class.

What are the limits of *Pride and Prejudice* as a period piece? How does our judgment of the characters Elizabeth Bennet and Fitzwilliam Darcy change when we put them in this larger social context? According to the sociological approach, you are justified in devaluing *Pride and Prejudice* because of its author's narrow, tendentious social views.

Generally speaking, if you emphasize the sociological in your report, you will be considering:

★ How well, and to what extent, does the author explain characters in terms of the social, economic, and biological conditions they have had to contend with?

★ How well, as part of his reponsibility to give us all relevant information, does the author create the total social environment in which his characters function?

Sociologically oriented literature tends to be about the lower classes and the contents tend to be surprising. Television, the movies, and advertising rarely give us any glimpse of the American working people. The spotlight is almost always on the upper classes. And so, when you read a novel like Chuck Wachtel's *Joe the Engineer*, the discoveries you make, the vicarious experiences you have of blue-collar life, might well determine the emphasis of your report. You might dwell, for example, on the shocking effects of a limited education on Joe's psyche.

The Psychological Emphasis

You might find yourself, sometimes at least, focusing more on the behavior of individual characters than on their relation to the larger social picture. You might wonder why it is that such a sensitive and wise person as Hamlet can be so oblivious to the plight of Ophelia. Why does Catherine in *Wuthering Heights* allow herself to be destroyed by what is, after all, only a human situation? Why does Heathcliff become such a monster after he is spurned?

While reading Milton's *Samson Agonistes*, you may think: How can all the men in this play be so blind to the fact that Dalila, whom they hold in contempt, has done nothing more than Samson, whom they honor? That is, Samson has *also* used sex for ulterior motives! You decide, in this case at least, that it's as much a social as a psychological question. Maybe it reveals as much about Milton's society as it does about Samson's. Excellent topics for book reports!

If you prefer to stress the psychological questions in literature, the *motivation* behind each character's deeds and moods, you are following one of the oldest traditions in criticism. Until the past century, the dramatist and the fiction writer were, in the popular mind at least, considered to be the main practitioners of psychological inquiry. *Hamlet* and *Wuthering Heights* have served as major texts for the study of behavior.

Creative writers no longer enjoy such a monopoly in psychology, and this change has had great consequences for both writers and readers. Largely taking their cues from literature, modern thinkers like Sigmund Freud and Carl Jung have developed "depth psychology." Just as Zola and his followers stress the outer, objective, social determinants of character, so the Freudian-Jungian school stresses the inner, unconscious, subjective forces that influence our behavior.

Freud sees man's psyche as the stage for a continuous conflict among his ego (conscious, social self), his id (unconscious mind), and his superego (deeply ingrained "conscience"). Jung sees additional components in the unconscious, which he divides into the personal and the collective; he sees, for example, an anima (a female component) in every man, an animus (a male component) in every woman. And Jung feels that every person must come to terms with his/her anima/animus, and with other "archetypes" at home in the unconscious before becoming a fully individual Self.

Post-Freudians have extended Freud's study of "the family (Oedipal) situation" into such questions as sibling rivalry, "the politics of the family," and the identity crisis.

In short, today's novelists, poets, and playwrights write for an audience already familiar with the concepts of Freud, Jung, Alfred Adler, Erich Fromm, R.D. Laing, and Eric Erikson. Just as today's readers expect today's writers to reflect Zolaist concerns with the social milieu, so they expect new fiction and drama to reflect our new knowledge of the darker, more mysterious side of human nature. Psychology is taught as early as the high school years, and popular paperback editions of psychoanalytic works are available to all.

So if you yourself lean toward a psychological interpretation in your reading, you should feel free, when writing your book reports, to use whatever formal psychology you can apply. It is easy these days for almost anyone to appreciate the Freudian aspects in Samuel Beckett's *Waiting for Godot* and Jungian features in Eugene O'Neill's *Emperor Jones* or in Joyce's *Finnegans Wake*. You would have little trouble showing that Hermann Hesse's *Demian* is a very straightforward translation into fiction of Jung's theory of personality.

It takes advanced knowledge to discuss the influence of R.D. Laing on Doris Lessing's *Briefing for a Descent into Hell*. Of course, you could be the naive layperson again, "discovering" the psychology in O'Neill and Lessing yourself, discussing its validity with no outside knowledge whatsoever of its background theory.

The Archetypal Emphasis

At some point in your schooling—perhaps when you studied T.S. Eliot's *The Waste Land*—you might have enjoyed the fact that a modern author, guided by anthropology, can make good artistic use of ancient myths. Whether you knew it by this word or not, you were becoming fascinated by *mythopoeia*, or the making and remaking of myths. In *The Waste Land*, for example, Eliot's protagonist imagines him/herself as the knight in Quest of the Holy Grail. Eliot goes further and blends elements from different religions. Throughout the five parts of *The Waste Land*, Eliot is thus able to contrast modern life with that of past epochs, to reveal the recurrent, the cyclic, and the universal. He intensifies his emotional effect because, in writing about today, he also taps our feelings associated with the great myths that survive from our past.

Thus, in reporting on James Joyce's *Ulysses*, a novel set in twentieth-century Dublin, you might want to stress the mythic parallel indicated by the title. You will enjoy comparing and contrasting the exploits of Homer's Telemachus, Odysseus (Ulysses), and Penelope with a day in the life of Joyce's Stephen Daedalus, Leopold Bloom, and Molly Bloom. Or you can examine the mythic underpinnings in Joseph Heller's *Catch-22*, John Updike's *The Centaur*, or Earl Shorris' *Under the Fifth Sun: A Novel of Pancho Villa*.

Your excitement in these investigations consists in your meeting such questions as:

★ Why did the author base the plot on this myth or his characters on these archetypes?

★ What is the significance of the way he departs from the myth?

★ What overall message is implicit in his mythopoeia?

★ If readers are not aware of the archetypal parallels, are they still affected by them emotionally?

Aspects Combined

You have, in other words, the option of using any of several possible approaches and emphases. Some of them allow you to bring an outside interest—

whether in surfcasting, psychology, or sociology—to bear on a literary work. But you could stress *any* of these aspects—the ideological, aesthetic, psychological, archetypal—without involving any specialized outside study.

If Didi and Gogo in Samuel Beckett's *Waiting for Godot* seem to you to represent the rational and the irrational parts of man's makeup, you can discuss that perception with no recourse to the Freudians. You will still have stressed the psychology behind Beckett's characterization. And you need no special knowledge of sociology to realize what Sinclair is doing when he takes impoverished Jurgis Rudkus through the mansion of a millionaire. You can enjoy making that point all by yourself.

Of course, you do not want to stress any *one* aspect to the exclusion of all others. Let's say you do prefer to emphasize the sociological aspects of Jurgis' situation. You would still not want to ignore Sinclair's artistry entirely. After all, it's his success in telling a story well that makes the sociological messages so effective. Conversely, if you want to concentrate mainly on his aesthetic strengths and weaknesses, you would still have to acknowledge that much of the power of the book comes from its journalistic revelations. And whether or not you choose to argue with Sinclair's ideology, you will still have to devote some space to his message.

More Specialized Knowledge

We have referred in passing to Racine as "neoclassicist," Brontë as "romanticist," Sinclair as "Zolaist," and to your own reactions, expressed in a book report, as possibly "impressionist." If we dwell on these terms for a few minutes, we will be able to add them to that growing body of specialized knowledge we said would help you write more and more sophisticated reports.

Classicism

Ancient Greek and Roman authors felt that the ideal literature would be characterized by a perfect balance of form and content, objectivity and subjectivity, the social and the personal, reason and emotion. A character who favored reason over emotion was as much "off balance" and out of touch with reality as a character who was more impulsive than rational. Classical authors themselves strove for such balance in their own writings. You may, in your book report, refer to an author who achieves this balance as CLASSICIST in his tone.

Neoclassicism

During the Age of Reason (roughly 1600–1800), the major writers believed they were successful in attaining the CLASSICIST ideal. They were NEOCLASSICISTS (new classicists). However, today we feel that in actuality they greatly favored reason, wit, form, conformity, and tradition over feeling, intuition, imagination, individualism, and innovation. We have already called Racine a neoclassicist. You should try out the word when you want to describe an author who exhibits strong logical, formal control over his feelings and imagination, and who seems to prefer the knowable to the mysterious, the objective to the subjective, contour to color.

Romanticism

In rebellion against the strictures of the Age of Reason, many writers, in the nineteenth century especially, favored individual emotion, intuition, imagination, and free forms over objective reasoning, social logic, and tight structure. They preferred the natural and the rural instead of the urban. We call them ROMANTICISTS. (The word grew out of the fact that some of their earliest impulses were expressed in the *roman,* or romance, an early type of novel.) Whenever you write about an author who, like Emily Brontë, freely acknowledges and explores the emotional life and the mysterious, you may call him/her a ROMANTICIST.

Naturalism

The literary philosophy of ZOLAISM, which we have discussed, is better known today as NATURALISM. This is the movement in art that stresses the extent to which man is shaped by biological and social forces. The NATURALIST believes that the writer must explore all aspects of life, no matter how unpleasant, disgusting, or "unliterary" some of them may be. You may distinguish a NATURALIST from a REALIST by this simple test: The REALIST holds up a mirror to real life, but only to selected parts of real life; for example, he will close the bathroom door and the bedroom door. But the NATURALIST records all of existence, following his characters everywhere life takes them. Try to decide whether the book you are reporting on is:

★ NATURALIST?   ★ REALIST?   ★ ROMANTICIST?
★ NEOCLASSICIST?   ★ CLASSICIST?

Impressionism

We said earlier that you are free simply to tell how the book *impresses* you, to give your own personal, naive, unprofessional reactions. This is the IMPRESSIONIST approach. An author is using such an approach in fiction when he limits our knowledge of what's going on to the way the world impresses itself on a single mind. A good example is Henry James' *What Maisie Knew.* We view all of the action through the mind of Maisie who is five to eight years old in the course of the story. What Maisie does not understand we must figure out for ourselves. When a writer constructs a work—book report or novel—exclusively out of the sensations recorded by one mind, the writer is using the IMPRESSIONIST technique.

Expressionism

The IMPRESSIONIST technique is one way of representing states of mind, specifically the way the outer world *impresses* itself upon that mind. Another psychological technique is EXPRESSIONISM. The author represents the character's state of mind as imposing itself on the outer world.

In Franz Kafka's "Metamorphosis," the main character is made to feel, by his boss and his parents, like an insect. He wakes up one morning to discover that he *is* a cockroach. Whenever you report on a work in which objective reality is distorted by a state of mind, call it EXPRESSIONIST.

You are now equipped with a rudimentary knowledge of:

★ what we have a right to expect from a book

★ typical approaches and emphases in book report writing

★ some basic terminology that we use to characterize different modes of literature

Let us now consider how further to analyze and evaluate first FICTION, then DRAMA, then POETRY, then NONFICTION. Finally, we shall come back to the question of how we organize our analysis and evaluation into a book report.

Chapter 2

How to Analyze and Evaluate Fiction

Working Statement of Theme
Plot
Characterization
Setting
Point of View
Style and Tone
Final Statement of Theme

HOW TO ANALYZE AND EVALUATE FICTION

When you finish reading a work of fiction, and you allow its overall effects to "sink in," you naturally, rather helplessly, begin to meditate along two lines of thought.

1. What is the overall effect of the work? What message does the author want me to get? What intellectual reactions have I had? What emotions has the author stirred up in me?

2. Since I'm going to write a book report on this work: How do I explain the effects, the impact? How did the author achieve them?

At the same time, then, as you mull over this vicarious experience you have had, you think about both *theme* and *techniques*. You realize you can formulate a casual, general statement about the theme early in your reflection. But a final, full, responsible statement of the author's message, his conclusions, might not be possible until you have thought more about his methods, the implicit as well as the explicit aspects of his work.

So you accept the fact that you can begin with only a *working statement of theme*, then you must explore fully the author's use of *plot*, *characterization*, *point of view*, *setting*, *style*, *tone*—and finally arrive at a more detailed, *conclusive statement* about his message.

Working Statement of Theme

Thus, with "The Freshest Boy" you might decide that the theme, generally speaking, is a boy's initiation into the realities of life, his acceptance of the responsibility to mold his own character.

With *The Jungle*, you realize that the theme, expressed in its most general terms, is in the title: In 1900–1904, industrial life in America is a *jungle* life, and something must be done to civilize it. It helps to keep the formulation simple until you reexamine the work more thoroughly.

Plot

You need no specialized knowledge to realize that the first technical aspect to consider is the story, the plot. Your book report must contain a succinct summary of the action.

Plot *vs.* Story

But as soon as you attempt to summarize the action, you begin to appreciate the fact that there really is a big difference between story and plot! *Story*, you realize, is the chronological order in which the events actually occurred. *Plot*, on the other hand, is a nonchronological order in which the author has decided to reveal those events.

As a simple example, we can consider "The Freshest Boy," comparing the *story*, or Fitzgerald's raw material, with his *plot*, or his artistically designed narrative.

Story: "The Freshest Boy"

Basil Lee and Lewis Crum both attended Country Day in a Midwestern city where their fathers were lifelong friends. Basil's mother was too lenient on him and he never learned how to work, study, or organize his life. Instead, he earned a reputation as a nuisance and was denounced in the school paper as an indiscreet loudmouth. Lewis was graduated a year ahead of Basil and was the first to go on to St. Regis School in the East.

The following year, as they were riding together on the train heading east, they got into an argument. Newcomer Basil was full of hopes and fantasies about his coming success in his new environment. Veteran Lewis, however, was pessimistic, stressing not only the negative aspects of his own first year at St. Regis, but also that Basil, in fact, had always been unpopular with his schoolmates.

Although Basil tried to live down that notoriety and turn over a new leaf, he soon found himself reliving his old role. Everyone at St. Regis disliked him as a conceited boaster, an officious critic of his fellow students. In a deep depression, he went to New York to escape into the dream world of a musical comedy.

A worshiper of celebrities, he hung around the stage entrance after the show. Following two of his favorites, a football hero and the star of the musical, he eavesdropped on their conversation in a restaurant. For the first time he understood that even successful people have to overcome personal difficulties.

Basil's indulgent mother offered him a chance to try another school, far away in Europe. He decided to stay at St. Regis and earn the respect of teachers and students. Through months of trials and errors he consoled himself by remembering the athlete and the actress. Then one day, playing basketball, he heard another ballplayer, who had once disliked Basil, call him by a gentle nickname. Basil finally slept well at St. Regis.

Plot: "The Freshest Boy"

But Fitzgerald does not follow chronology. He begins his *plot* with a fantasy that Basil is having while the train is crossing Indiana. All the information we have given in the first paragraph of *our* summary of the story, Fitzgerald weaves into the conversation on the train and in subsequent scenes.

This is a simple example of how a professional fiction writer plays with time. Fitzgerald plunges us into the middle of things (*in medias res*), into a scene so contrived as to roll the action forward even while it unravels the past. Thus, while Basil and Lewis argue about what lies *ahead* of them, we learn much of what we have to know about what lies *behind* them.

Now let us look at the situation in *The Jungle*, a more complicated example of the difference between story and plot.

Story: *The Jungle*

Jurgis and his fiancée, Ona, lived with their families in Lithuania in the 1890s. They enjoyed their village life, dwelled in sturdy houses, ate natural foods, worked outdoors, but they were oppressed by the upper classes. Recruiters from America told them that high-paying jobs awaited them in Chicago, and there everyone would be equal and free.

The two families, including six children, embarked for America. In New York, they were cheated by officials; in Chicago, they lived in the filthiest rooming house they had ever seen. But the adults finally all got jobs in the packing plants, signed a mortgage for a "new" house, and gaily planned for the wedding of Jurgis and Ona.

Soon they were totally disillusioned by the dangerous working conditions, the packing of impure meats, the graft that pervaded industrial and civic life, and the discovery that their real estate agent had sold them a flimsy old house as new and had concealed the true costs, hoping they would fail to meet their payments and be dispossessed. They were forced to send Ona and even the children out to work.

When Ona and Jurgis were finally married, they were already deeply in debt. Work hazards and contaminated food killed two of their household, and Ona, after becoming a mother, was forced to serve as her boss' mistress, otherwise he would have had all her family fired. When Jurgis heard of Ona's infidelity, he attacked her boss; he was jailed, and they all lost their jobs and their house.

Jurgis left prison to find Ona dying in premature childbirth. After his son died in a street accident, Jurgis, blacklisted and unemployed, drifted. Forced to beg, he accidentally got a big bill from a rich man, was cheated out of it by a bartender, fought back and went back to jail. Through his prison contacts, after his release he wandered into crime and became a strikebreaker. For the first time, he enjoyed real money. But meeting Ona's boss, he attacked him again and was imprisoned again.

A "free" man, Jurgis stumbled into a Socialist meeting and heard a speech that summed up American working-class life exactly as he had known it. Converted to the Socialist mission of building a democratic society in which industry would be owned by the people, he helped the Socialists rack up a record vote in Chicago in 1904.

Plot: *The Jungle*

Instead of telling this story in chronological order, Sinclair invented a plot. He opens his novel *in medias res* at the wedding feast. This happiest event in the lives of Jurgis and Ona gives Sinclair his best chance to introduce most of his characters and their situation as immigrants in America. Then, in Chapter 2, he starts a series of flashbacks that give us the two families' history in the Lithuanian forest and the American jungle. In Chapter 7, he picks up the story where he had left off at the end of Chapter 1. From Chapters 7 to 31, he uses continuous action with flashbacks, the most important being Ona's explanation to Jurgis how her affair with her boss had begun many weeks earlier.

Thus Sinclair and Fitzgerald, like most authors, have eschewed chronology and instead have rearranged the order of events. For them, plot is a device for unfolding a story in a more dramatic and suspenseful fashion. For their readers, plot is the means by which they slowly discover and put together the pieces of the complete story.

Plot: Overall Structure

Your first task in analyzing the action, then, is to distinguish the story from the plot and to explain how the plot enhances the story. All the background information about Basil's life in the Midwest, and about Jurgis' in Lithuania, would have provided a boring introduction to the main action. So, in each case, the author plunged into the middle of his story. He starts at the point where his characters are already in transition, soon to be off-balance and in conflict. He correctly assumes that once you and I sympathize with people off-balance, we will be more tolerant of background information.

That section of his story in which the author must introduce his characters and explain their background situation is called the *exposition*. How well an author handles his exposition will be one of your main concerns in evaluating his plot.

In a well-plotted story, the conflict begins as early as possible, sometimes even before the exposition. That point where the conflict is definitely underway is called *the initial moment*. In "The Freshest Boy," the initial moment comes when Basil is reminded of his history, a history of habits that could destroy his dreams of success. In *The Jungle*, the initial moment comes when newlyweds Jurgis and Ona realize they have been cheated at their wedding: They start off married life not with a comfortable "nest egg" but with staggering debts.

In both cases, the author has allowed us a good look at the characters in a state of happiness, of equilibrium, before the conflict begins. Basil enjoys his fantasy on the train, Jurgis and Ona enjoy the dancing and feasting, all before the threat of unhappiness, of disequilibrium, is introduced. You will see that such a pattern is essential to the plot.

If you write a report, for example, on Barbara Girion's *A Tangle of Roots*, you will find this inevitable contrast. Beth is quite content in school, facing no bigger problems than keeping up her grades, working on the yearbook, and choosing the right bra. Then the principal calls her down to his office. "Beth, there's no easy way to tell you. Your mother's dead."

The initial moment. The conflict begins. How can Beth live without a mother? What will happen to her father? How will they face their new personal and common problems?

As soon as the characters tackle their new situations, we realize that their conflicts are *inner* as well as *outer*. Basil has to face not only a new school situation, he has to cope with old personal weaknesses. Jurgis must contend not only with a cruel system intent on exploiting him but also with his own naive, blind faith that anyone who works hard will inevitably earn what he deserves. Can Beth develop the inner strength to survive without a mother?

After the *exposition* and *initial moment*, the author creates selected incidents to demonstrate how the characters are coming to grips with their problems. Fitzgerald uses a November school day to show us that Basil is already rejected and apparently defeated. Sinclair takes us through a series of adventures, industrial and domestic, as most of the characters fall by the wayside and only Jurgis survives—barely so. This part of the plot is known as the *complication* or *rising action*.

In a short story, the rising action will usually culminate in a single *crisis*, or a turning point. Thus, Basil overhears a conversation which gives him the insight he needs to resolve his own inner conflict and to tackle his outer conflict anew.

In a novel there will be a series of crises until the character faces the final crisis. When Jurgis joins the union, for example, we have reached a minor turning point in the action; when he attacks Ona's boss, we are approaching a major crisis. The most decisive point in his life comes when his bitter experience makes it possible for him to make the intellectual connection between his own plight and the social doctrine he hears from a political speaker.

The crisis, especially the major crisis, is likely to be drawn out and agonizing. That moment when a crisis hits its peak of intensity is called the *climax*. The crisis in "The Freshest Boy," begins when Basil understands that even great celebrities must constantly cope with personal problems, "that life for everybody was a struggle." Leaving the restaurant and walking along Broadway, Basil slowly lets the lesson sink in until finally he applies it to his own problems at St. Regis.

We see how he has become a new person, a person of definite resolve, when he finds his teacher, Mr. Rooney, drunk in a bar:

> "You got to come with me into the washroom and get cleaned up, and then you can sleep on the train again, Mr. Rooney. Come on, Mr. Rooney, please . . ."

Suddenly, Basil has taken on adult responsibilities! The *insights* he has gained have been converted into *action*; his *crisis* has reached its *climax*.

A similar pattern can be found in *The Jungle*. The final crisis begins when Jurgis wildly senses that the speaker has the answers to Jurgis' problems. But Sinclair again puts Jurgis into conflict. An unkempt tramp, Jurgis wonders whether he dare introduce himself to this great orator. He finally overcomes his doubts and shyness, volunteers to join the movement—and is accepted!

Some further action after such a climax is needed to show the resolution of the hero's situation as a result of the crisis ordeal. This is often called the *denouement* or *falling action*. The main problem is resolved; the tension is relaxed. For his falling action, Fitzgerald uses a February scene on a basketball court. For his, Sinclair portrays Jurgis in new circumstances, devoted again to a life he can believe in, working with people of high ideals who hold him in respect.

Plot, then, is a mechanism which takes characters through three major stages and two major changes. In the first stage, we see characters in a state of equilibrium. In the second, we see them thrown off balance, facing a new conflict. In the third, we see them resolve the conflict for better or worse, either emerging triumphant or going down to defeat. The first stage is precipitated into the second by the initial moment. The second is changed into the third by the climax.

In other words, *plot is an arrangement of events in which characters are tested by circumstances, challenged to change either the situation or themselves or both.*

Plot: Other Considerations

When you have identified the expository elements, the initial moment and the crisis, the rising and falling action, you have mapped out the overall structure of your assigned work of fiction. Now you might consider how the author keeps his action moving through this overall structure.

Suspense

Structure can be seen as the creation and satisfaction of curiosity. At every stage of his work the author must create suspense over new questions and problems, satisfy us with some answers and solutions, and lead us to still other questions.

At one point in *The Jungle,* the question is whether Jurgis can find a job, later whether his father can. Such problems solved, a new one emerges: Can they find better housing and, once they sign the mortgage, can they pay it off? When we are inside the prison cell with Jurgis, we wonder, what's happening to the others? When Sinclair follows Jurgis in his hoboing around the country, Sinclair keeps us in suspense about Marija and the children. What's happening to them back in the city?

One of the longest passages of suspense in *Wuthering Heights* begins when Catherine is confiding in Nelly about her feelings toward Heathcliff and her fiancé. Has Heathcliff overheard? If so, how much, up to what point in Catherine's account? Has this had anything to do with his disappearance? All during Catherine's illness, recovery, and early marriage, we wonder, will Heathcliff return? When he does, a new problem arises: How will Catherine's husband's sister respond to him?

Ebb and Flow

To intensify suspense, keep the story unpredictable, and simulate real life, an author represents his characters' fortunes and moods as alternating in an ebb-and-flow pattern.

In Chapter 5 of *The Jungle,* all the characters are happy in their "nest feathering." Then all the wage earners in the house face a staggering series of disillusionments. In Chapter 20, Jurgis decides he must carry on for the sake of his now motherless boy. He tries to get work but discovers that the packers have blacklisted him. Seemingly doomed to the hand-to-mouth existence of an errand boy, he meets an old friend who gets him a job in the harvester works. Jurgis once again is full of hope for education in night school, advancement, and security. Then one day his department suspends operations "until further notice."

Scene-Summary-Scene

Another pattern authors use in order to change the pace and the focus, and to speed up the action, is alternation of scene and summary. A *scene* dramatizes a single event, as when Fitzgerald zooms in on the athlete, the actress, and the eavesdropper, giving us dialogue, gestures, specific details. A *summary* swiftly condenses a lot of action, occurring over a relatively long period of time, into a few compact, general statements, such as:

> It was a long hard time. Basil got on bounds again in December and wasn't free again until March. An indulgent mother had given him no habits of work and this was almost beyond the power of anything but life itself to remedy, but he made numberless new starts and failed and tried again.

Notice, in a scene the author *shows*; in a summary, he *tells*. Fitzgerald unfolds "The Freshest Boy" in four dramatized scenes that alternate with narrated summaries. Modern readers prefer scenes and so authors keep summaries as brief, compact, and suspenseful as possible.

Sinclair repeatedly divides his chapters according to this scene-summary-scene pattern. He opens Chapter 15 with an introductory summary, briefly telling us that the wage earners are working sixteen hours a day during the rush season and that Jurgis senses something is happening in Ona's life that she cannot talk about. Now Sinclair stages a full, extended scene, with dialogue and detailed action: One night shortly before Thanksgiving, Ona does not come home from work. The next morning she explains that she has stayed with a friend because, during the fierce weather, the trolley "cars had stopped running."

Sinclair now switches to transitional summary: The heavy cold lasts for a month; morning after morning, Jurgis has had to half-carry Ona to work. Now Sinclair slows down and zooms in for another fully developed scene: Once again Ona fails to come home. In the morning Jurgis goes to her friend's house only to learn that Ona has never stayed there. When Ona does return, Jurgis, in a long, passionate dialogue, forces the truth out of her. Her boss intimidated her into becoming his mistress by threatening to have them all—Jurgis, Ona, her mother and sister, even the children—fired if she does not give herself to him. Jurgis rushes out of the house. In the trolley, the other passengers see him as a wild animal. He bursts into the place where Ona works and attacks her boss; Jurgis is dragged off to jail.

Action-Thought-Action

Another natural pattern that fiction writers use is alternation of action and thought. A good example is Sinclair's Chapter 16. Dumped into jail, Jurgis has plenty of time to reconsider his actions; to realize the damage he has done: they will now all lose their jobs and their house; to imagine the sufferings he has caused. Then Sinclair switches to action as Jurgis is taken before a magistrate, found unable to put up bail, and remanded to jail.

There he does his first serious thinking. He decides that justice is a lie; the packers have "bought the law," murdered his father, abused his wife, and cowed them all. Sinclair thus uses a thought-phase in the action-thought cycle to arrive at the first major crisis of *The Jungle*. This is the beginning of Jurgis' rebellion.

Evaluating Plot

You now have the main concepts, with appropriate terminology, for discussing an author's handling of plot:

☆ How does he rearrange the events of the basic chronological story? How does this rearrangement enhance the story? the reader's interest? the suspense?

☆ How does the author solve the difficulties of exposition? Does he supply necessary background information in a boring or in a graceful manner?

☆ Is the initial moment convincing? Does it involve the reader in a credible conflict?

☆ Does the author develop the story mainly through fully developed scenes, with the characters talking? Or does he rely heavily on lengthy narration, with the author talking?

☆ Do crisis, climax, and resolution grow naturally out of previous situations? Are they credible? For example, some critics of *The Jungle* feel that it simply is not believable that Jurgis, reduced to the status of a down-and-out bum, could be inspired and rejuvenated by a speech.

☆ Your overall considerations: Has the author designed a plot that adequately reveals, explores, and tests the characters? What does the plot contribute to the theme?

But suppose the fiction seems "plotless," that is, structured differently from the way we described plot here. For a different approach to structure, then, see the section on Plot in the chapter "How to Analyze and Evaluate Drama" (pages 58–66). Refer especially to the sections entitled "Two Types of Plot" (page 58) and "Nontraditional Dramatic Structure" (page 64).

Characterization

You see it now: Works of fiction like "The Freshest Boy" and *The Jungle* are stories only because a character or characters have undergone profound change. Without some such radical developments, we just don't have a story. That kind of change in personality, and the author's methods for accounting for it, are what we call *characterization*.

And, of course, plot and characterization are just two aspects of the same phenomenon. They can be discussed only in terms of each other. Plot is the sequence of events that tests and reveals character; character in turn initiates events. When we talk of plot, as we did in the preceding section, we emphasize *what* the characters do; when we discuss characterization, as we shall here in depth, we emphasize *why* they do it.

Your main concern, your key word, then, in analyzing character is *motivation*. What is it in a character's temperament, background, experience, and orientation that *motivates* him/her to act as he/she does?

Classification of Characters

You will find certain other standard terms useful in discussing character; they make it easier for you to keep in mind what critics and readers expect of fiction writers.

Major and Minor Characters

Main characters are those so central to the action, so continual in their presence, that we expect that the author will explore their makeup and motivation most thoroughly. If one main character is studied far more than any other, we may call him/her the *focus character* or the *protagonist*.

Jurgis is a perfect example. He is the only character in *The Jungle* to figure in every chapter; we see most of the action and other characters mainly through his experience. His wife Ona is also a main character, and we could make a case for calling Ona's cousin Marija a major character too because of the role she plays in the action and because of the care Sinclair takes to understand her changes in values.

By comparison, all the others in *The Jungle* are *minor characters.* They number about sixty identifiable people and scores of unidentified ones. They are seen by us only as they impinge on the lives of the central persons in the action. Indeed, we may see the minor characters only as the major characters see them. Characters are *major* or *minor,* then, according to their distance from the central character(s) in the story.

This corresponds to our perception in real life. You are *the* central character, the focus in your own life. Other main characters are, perhaps, your parents, other close relatives, perhaps a certain teacher or friend. Beyond them is a vast cast of minor characters: people you interact with at only one period in your life, or just occasionally, some of them known to you only through others, some not even known to you by name.

Round and Flat Characters

A more critical way of classifying characters is that introduced by the famous English novelist E.M. Forster. In his *Aspects of the Novel*, he divides fictional people into *round* and *flat* characters.

A *round* character is so called because he/she has *depth*. The author's characterization is *complex* and *dynamic*, that is, the character changes and the changes are accounted for.

In *The Jungle*, for example, Marija is first seen as an immigrant woman who believes that hard work and virtue will bring her security and happiness in America. By the end of the novel, she is thoroughly disillusioned with traditional values, supporting herself and her dependents on her earnings as a prostitute. She has discovered that, for the working class, only impropriety pays off.

Upton Sinclair not only carefully details the stages of Marija's change, he assigns himself the task of making Jurgis understand it: Jurgis who was also a proponent of the work ethic, Jurgis who was intolerant of his wife when she was forced to yield her virtue to her boss. Marija is many-sided, and we know her both from the outside and the inside, always in transition.

By contrast, the *flat* character is known to us only from one side, the side that he presents to the main characters. Thus all we know of "Bush" Harper, a labor spy and underworld figure, is the way he appears and reappears in Jurgis' life: to recruit and reward him for some illegal activity. We see only the sinister and corrupt side of "Bush" with no chance to understand how he got that way, no chance to see whatever "good" side he may have. Static and simple, he is the perfect *flat* character.

Forster's terminology helps us express judgments of an author's characterizations. For example, we expect that a main character will be *round*. It's a serious negative criticism if a reader can say that a major character is *flat*.

Indeed, here we have our main criterion for distinguishing serious literature from trash. Superior fiction offers us main characters who are *complex, dynamic, round* characters. Inferior fiction features main characters who are *simple, static, flat*.

Naturally, we expect that even in serious fiction some or most of the minor characters will be seen as flat: we do not spend enough time with them to see them in the round. It's a surprise, then, a point in the author's favor, if you discover minor characters who are fairly well-rounded.

If you were reporting on *The Jungle*, you might well praise Sinclair for his depiction of Madame Haupt, the midwife. She appears in only two scenes, yet she comes so vigorously alive that we feel we know her well. It's only an illusion, but a happy one; she is a flat character but a colorful one.

The Type

Long before Forster, critics talked of characters who are *types*. A type has no individuality to speak of. When he shows us only one side of himself, it's the same side that many other characters have shown us in the history of literature. Thus we recognize the braggart soldier, the nagging wife, the henpecked husband, the Don Juan, the prostitute with a heart of gold, the comic sidekick, and so on. Using Forsterian terminology, we could call the *type* the *flattest* of the flat characters.

Again, to say that an author uses a *type* is a negative criticism only if it is a main character who is so cast. For in real life, we tend to see many persons, especially at a distance, as types: the absent-minded professor, for example, or the "macho" motorcycle rider are likely to seem like types until we get to know them better.

You will find that an author is using a type for valid literary purposes when he/she is trying to make a generalization about a group. Thus, in his depiction of Mike Scully, Sinclair deliberately creates a composite figure of leading corrupt political bosses of the day. And in portraying Freddie Jones, son of a packing tycoon, Sinclair wants us to consider how *all* such "idle rich" spend their time.

The Archetype

You will realize too in your reading that often an author is trying to create a special kind of type known as an *archetype*. An *archetype* is a projection of our own psychological needs. Thus, in Hermann Hesse's *Demian*, Emil Sinclair sees Eva as a mother figure, indeed as the Earth Goddess, Eve, "the mother of all things." We see her only as Emil sees her, not as she indeed may appear to others without his need.

An ordinary type exists to help us classify a character in a simple way. But an archetype exists as a powerful psychological influence on the other characters and, the author hopes, on the reader too.

Sympathetic Characters

A final useful distinction can be made between *sympathetic* and *unsympathetic* characters. Usually we want to identify with at least one character if we are going to have that vicarious experience so vital to our enjoyment of literature. This character must be somewhat likable and understandable, a fair mix of strengths and weaknesses that seem credible and human and so can enlist our sympathy.

Usually the main character must be sympathetic. We like Jurgis for his strength, his honesty, even as we deplore his naivete; since we all have our own blind spots, we can sympathize with his efforts to overcome his. Minor characters may or may not be sympathetic. Madame Haupt, although gross, is sympathetic, while Mike Scully is not. If we do happen to identify with an unlikable, evil person like Scully, we probably do so unconsciously, allowing the darker side of our nature to explore evil vicariously. Of course, the consciously moral side of us wants to see the evil character defeated. But until he is, we have experienced evil in a safe and informative way.

Methods of Characterization

In your book report, you may want to comment on any or all of the five methods of characterization your author may use.

Authorial Description

The first, easiest, and often the least artistic, is for the author him/herself to tell us what the characters are like, what they are feeling, maybe even what the author thinks of them! Thus Fitzgerald tells us:

> His [Basil's] bright dark-blue eyes were at this moment fixed upon his companion with boredom and impatience.

And Sinclair:

> She [Ona] was so young—not quite sixteen—and small for her age, a mere child; and she had just been married . . . to Jurgis, of all men, . . . he with the mighty shoulders and the giant hands.
>
> Ona was blue-eyed and fair, while Jurgis had great black eyes with beetling brows, and thick black hair that curled in waves about his ears—in short, they were one of those incongruous and impossible married couples with which Mother Nature so often wills to confound all prophets. . . .

We've called this the least "artistic" method because the author is not, at this point at least, letting the characters reveal themselves, and, in Sinclair's case, he is heavily editorializing. It would have been much more dramatic if Ona and Jurgis could be seen through the eyes of another character. And Sinclair's imposing such judgments of the characters on us lessens our chances of coming to our own conclusions.

Now such direct commentary is inevitable if the author is telling the story from his/her point of view. Fitzgerald uses such authorial observations judiciously, sparingly, to speed up the action, and blends them with a greater proportion of action and dialogue. Sinclair, however, intrudes the authorial presence more than he has to.

In your book report, then, you might consider the degree to which the author intrudes and the value of his absence or presence.

Description by Other Characters

A second way for the author to depict character, as we have suggested, is to let us know how other characters react to him/her.

"I guess everybody knows," Lewis Crum reminds Basil, "you were the freshest boy at Country Day."

Stated by a character, in a nasty way, this is far more dramatic than if it had been related by the author. An author's statements seem godlike and final; a character's may be tentative, subjective, totally wrong, more revealing of the person speaking them than of the person spoken of. Thus, one character's description of another can be more suspenseful, more suggestive of conflict, than similar remarks made by the author.

Change of personality, as we have emphasized, is the very stuff of fiction. *Having one character react to change in another is a very rapid and credible way of convincing the reader.* Thus Emily Brontë, in *Wuthering Heights*, has Nelly tell Mr. Lockwood how she was

amazed . . . to behold the transformation of Heathcliff. He had grown [into] a tall, athletic, well-formed man . . . His upright carriage suggested the idea of his having been in the army. His countenance . . . looked intelligent, and retained no marks of former degradation.

Character's Self-Image

The third method is for the author to let us know what a character thinks of himself and, equally important, *how* he thinks, generally. He may be wrong in his self-judgment, but that becomes an important part of his characterization. Some of Basil's specific faults, like his nagging his schoolmates about their weaknesses, and some of his biggest problems, like his relative poverty, we discover only through his own self-analysis. His internal monologue is one of the reasons we know he can grow.

The way Jurgis' self-image changes is one of the highlights of Sinclair's characterization. At the beginning, Jurgis believes that with his superior strength, his willingness always to "work harder," he will succeed when others fail. Later, in prison, he looks back on this self-confidence as naive. He sees now that he was a blind, pathetic fool, a victim of ruthless employers. A character's current self-image can be a reliable source of suspense and irony. Making good money as a political dirty-worker, for example, Jurgis deceives himself that this is happiness, this is what he was meant for.

A character's pattern of thought can be as revealing as the subjects he dwells on. For example, in reading Jules Verne's *Twenty Thousand Leagues under the Sea*, you would note not only the questions that Professor Aronnax reflects on. You would sense too how he is a thorough, methodical, logical thinker, indeed almost obsessively so.

Action

The fourth, most important means of characterization available to the author is showing his/her character in action. We know Basil has learned a lesson, gained new moral strength, because he assumes some responsibility when he finds Mr. Rooney in a helpless state. We know Jurgis is self-sacrificing when, to save his dependents from hunger, he is willing to take the most hazardous, most humiliating job of all. He becomes a fertilizer worker and literally earns the nickname "The Stinker." We know that Jurgis is on the verge of rebellion when he uproots a selfish farmer's newly planted trees.

Action involves choices and choices reveal character. Basil's mother gives him an out: he can escape to Europe. But he decides to stay at St. Regis and change his schoolfellows' jeers to cheers. Jurgis could enjoy the orator's speech and then relapse into despair. But he decides to give life one more chance, to see if there can truly be an altruistic, humanitarian leader that an honest man can follow.

Dialogue

Putting characters into action involves letting them talk, and, of course, dialogue is the essence of drama, as characters probe into each other's meanings and motives, incidentally revealing themselves.

> "What do you want?" Basil demanded.
> "Hold your horses, Bossy."
> Basil jumped to his feet. The little boy retreated a step.
> "Go on, hit me!" he chirped nervously. "Go on, hit me, 'cause I'm just half your size—Bossy."

Dialogue reveals—and elicits—character not only because of *what* is said but because of *how* it is said. An artistic author sees to it that each character has his/her own characteristic speech rhythms, diction, and figures of speech. One character will speak in long sentences full of generalities to another who talks in short bursts of colorful, concrete language. One character will sound as if he is delivering carefully prepared speeches while another sounds as if she is working out her ideas spontaneously as she talks. Such differences are significant to you as you seek clues to the portrayal of personality.

Foils

A fifth technique of characterization is the use of foils. The term *foil* is taken from the jeweler's trade. The jeweler will place a sheet of foil behind a gem in order to enhance it, or bring out its qualities. Thus Sinclair uses Marija as a foil for several characters.

Since Marija is vigorous, active, and powerful, she serves as a foil for the frail, passive Ona. Since she can command higher pay than Jurgis, she serves to highlight the absurdity of his belief in male supremacy. Since she, like Jurgis, believes that hard work and virtue will be rewarded, her fate seems to enhance his. She goes down to defeat, turning to prostitution as the only way out, while he rises above circumstances and takes his fate into his own hands.

Evaluating Characterization

Getting set to discuss how your author portrays his characters you might consider:

☆ How does he *reveal* their makeup? How does he prepare us for their behavior, that is, how (and how well) does he supply *motivation* for their actions?

☆ Do the main characters *grow* or otherwise *change*? What can we infer is the *significance of the change* in character?

☆ How well does the author use certain characters as *foils,* that is, to enhance other characters? What is each character's *function* in the plot?

☆ What do we learn from the characterization about the *human condition*? To what extent can these matters be explained in traditional literary terms?

Applying what you have learned so far to, for example, *Twenty Thousand Leagues under the Sea,* you might take notes about the characters somewhat like this:

Conseil

Through his own action and speech, and through descriptions by others, Conseil is revealed as the blindly faithful servant of Professor Aronnax. For example, when his master is swept overboard, Conseil leaps into the sea after him. Conseil is witty, urbane, and smugly deferential. We learn almost nothing of his history and he changes not at all. His motivation is simple: For some psychological and economic reasons not discussed, he needs to devote his life to a master and to maintain his own self-image as the perfect servant. He flourishes in the security of being the permanent assistant. His name means *counsel*, which is ironic, because he listens more than he advises.

His main functions in the plot are the classic functions of the servant in literature: to give his master endless opportunity to air his views (for the reader's benefit), occasionally to ask questions that the author wants answered, and to provide humor as the "comic sidekick." In short, Conseil is a *flat* character, *static* and *simple*. He is the flattest of the flats, the *type*: a *stock character*. Indeed, it may be said that Conseil *wants* to be a type!

Ned Land

Through his own action and speech (we never get inside the thoughts of Conseil or Ned), and through descriptions by others, this harpooner is shown to be courageous, freedom-loving, expert in practical affairs, intelligent but not intellectual. He suffers few inner conflicts. His motivation is simple: Because he loves to practice his trade out on the wide sea as a free man, he wants desperately to escape from Captain Nemo's submarine. He is a *simple, sympathetic, flat* character, but *not* a type. He is his own person.

He serves as a *foil* to two other characters: His uncompromising love of freedom and his love of decisive action enhance by contrast the Professor's willingness to compromise and his love of deliberation and reflection. And Ned's great brawn, without equivalent brain, serves to enhance, by comparison and contrast, the great brawn *with* great brain of Captain Nemo.

Professor Aronnax

He is the most fully realized character, revealed through action, speech, *and* internal monologue: As the narrator of the story, he is the only one whose unspoken thoughts are accessible to the reader. Warm, compassionate, erudite, an Age of Reason scientist, he is still capable of naive Romanticist impressions and reactions. Knowledge, insight, and friendship are more precious to him than power and wealth.

His *motivations* are complex and result in agonizing conflicts. On the one hand, as a marine scientist now a prisoner on board Nemo's craft, Aronnax has the greatest opportunities ever to study underwater life and hence to revise and perfect his standard treatise on the subject. Furthermore, Nemo is one of the great geniuses of all time and Aronnax regards collaboration with Nemo to be a psychological as well as scientific benefit. On the other hand, Aronnax gradually realizes that Nemo is guilty of atrocities in some secret private war. Finally, the Professor loves his friend Land and cannot bear to see him kept on board against his will. Thus Aronnax is forced to separate, and then to choose between, scientific advantage and human rights. He (and so Conseil too!) rejects Nemo and escapes with Ned. Clearly, Aronnax has struggled through a major identity crisis and emerges a far more complex and mature person. He is a *sympathetic, dynamic, round* character.

Nemo

Through careful attention to Nemo's actions and conversations, Professor Aronnax demonstrates that the Captain is an engineering genius, a scientific investigator of the first magnitude, a moody devotee of the arts, an active and bold worker for political freedom everywhere. But some mysterious calamity has hit Nemo, inspiring in him two fierce obsessive drives: one, to enjoy his own anarchistic freedom in the sea, far from the tyrannies of land; the other, to wreak vengeance on the ships of a certain hated nation, which apparently destroyed his family. Nemo is thus in perpetual conflict. He is now the serene, creative student of nature and advocate of mankind, then suddenly the destructive avenger. But he grows morally, and partly redeems himself in our eyes, when, after sinking one more enemy warship, he yields to remorse, loses control of his submarine, and goes down into the maelstrom.

Nemo is *complex, dynamic, round*—indeed the *focal* character. But he is also modeled partly on a type and seen by Aronnax as an archetype. He is one more variant of the Byronic hero — the talented but misunderstood, disillusioned, exiled Romantic. And for the Professor, Nemo has the additional fascination of seeming to be what depth psychology now calls "the archetypal perfect father."

Significance of Characterization

The resolution of the characters' struggles shows that Verne (1) was well aware of an old human problem: seeking retaliation on an ugly, evil enemy can make the avenger ugly and evil, and (2) he was anticipating a modern problem: conducting scientific research under dubious auspices can have strong antihumanitarian implications.

Characterization and Theme

In other words, the way *situation* and *characterization* are resolved may actually point toward the *theme* of the story.

Setting

You will find that an author's use of setting may be more subtle than his advancement of plot and characterization. An author is well aware that you concentrate on action and allow setting to influence you indirectly, subliminally, literally as background. Only when you consciously analyze the effects of setting do you realize how all-pervasive its effects can be.

Setting helps establish *verisimilitude*. It can create *suspense* and *mood*. It can influence the *makeup* of a character. It can provide many of the *problems* that test character. Setting often takes on such deep psychological significance that it can become a major form of *symbolism*. Like plot and characterization, setting can point toward *theme*. And of course, when it is well described, setting can provide pleasure in its own right.

Setting: Verisimilitude

An author must make us accept the world he or she creates on its own terms. As swiftly as possible, he must make it plausible, make us comfortable in it. Samuel Taylor Coleridge gave us the classic expression for this process as it occurs in the reader's mind: He called it the "willing suspension of disbelief." The reader waits for all the help he can get to abandon his objective knowledge that the fictional is not the real, to settle down into the fiction as an alternate reality.

The author's rooting of the story in time and place—giving it a setting—is one of his/her main methods of achieving *verisimilitude*, or the appearance of reality. Notice how swiftly Fitzgerald is able to set his scene:

> Basil Lee's glazed eyes returned from the barns and billboards of the Indiana countryside to the interior of the Broadway Limited. The hypnosis of the swift telegraph poles faded and Lewis Crum's stolid face took shape against the white slip-cover of the opposite bench.

Fitzgerald has not only offered suggestive details to sketch the outside and inside scene; he has represented their psychological effect on a mind. Thus we are sensuously involved ourselves, willing to suspend our disbelief. We follow Basil from scene to scene, believing in the action because it is always unfolding in a place we see, hear, taste, touch, and even smell:

> He traversed a long corridor, muggy with that odor best described as the smell of stale caramels that is so peculiar to boys' schools, ascended a stairs and knocked at an unexceptionable but formidable door.

We believe in this particular railroad car, this particular hall, because the author uses our experience with familiar sensations to focus on, and make us understand, an unfamiliar situation. It has often been pointed out that we believe the witch exists because the author shows her riding on a real broom through real night air, under a real moon, over a real church spire.

Setting: Suspense and Mood

The predicament the characters are caught in provides, of course, the main element of suspense. Off balance with the characters, we want them to regain their balance so we can regain ours. And by blending predicament with certain aspects of the environment, the author can enhance that suspense. Thus, when Mr. Lockwood is already uncomfortable because Heathcliff has greeted him in an unfriendly manner, he cannot help making some connections with the setting:

> Wuthering Heights is the name of Mr. Heathcliff's dwelling. "Wuthering" being a significant provincial adjective, descriptive of the atmosphere's tumult to which its station is exposed in stormy weather. Pure, bracing ventilation they must have up there at all times, indeed; one may guess the power of the north wind blowing over the edge, by the excessive slant of a few stunted firs at the end of the house; and by a range of gaunt thorns all stretching their limbs one way, as if craving alms of the sun.

Brontë's description of the landscape, as viewed through a character's mind, helps create a mood of apprehensiveness and suspense; we wonder rather uneasily what goes on in such a wind-beaten place.

How his characters discover a strange environment is also one of Sinclair's main devices for achieving verisimilitude, suspense, and mood:

> A full hour before the party reached the city they had begun to note the perplexing changes in the atmosphere. It grew darker all the time, and upon the earth the grass seemed to grow less green. Every minute, as the train sped on, the colors of things became dingier; the fields were . . . parched and yellow, the landscape hideous and bare. And along with the thickening smoke they began to notice . . . a strange, pungent odor . . . some might have called it sickening. . . . Now, sitting in the trolley car, they realized that they were on their way to the home of it—that they had travelled all the way from Lithuania to it. . . . Then the party became aware of another strange thing. . . . a sound made up of ten thousand little sounds. . . .

Setting: Characterization

Here we see how, beyond creating suspense and rooting the action in a believable world of sense perceptions, the setting can loom as a test of character. From these early, disconcerting glimpses of their new environment through to the end of the novel, Sinclair's characters must continually cope with a physical world they themselves never made. Still too poor to own a raincoat, Ona comes down with a cold because of storms she must battle to get to work. Jurgis' father, so eager to get a job that he accepts one with terrible working conditions, is forced to stand in chemicals that rot his feet. Jurgis himself, working on blood-slippery floors of packing plants, is unable to get out of the way when a bull breaks loose and runs amok. Rains flood the slum area where Jurgis lives, turning the street into a canal, and Jurgis' little boy falls in and drowns.

But when Jurgis flees to the country, his health improves and he feels human again in the face of Nature. Setting is so important that it can—and does—change not only mood but even character. And different settings can create different characters. Sinclair intends us to infer that Freddie Jones, growing up in a luxurious mansion, has far more opportunity to succeed than does Jurgis, shivering in a cold house he shares with vermin no expensive insecticides can eliminate. Jurgis and his family are brutalized largely by the setting in which their economic circumstances force them to live.

Setting challenges not only physical but mental strength. When Nemo's submarine is trapped beneath the ice, the crew and their prisoners are forced to work against time, hacking away at the frozen surfaces around them as their oxygen supply diminishes. All their physical courage would be to no avail if the situation did not challenge Nemo's scientific ingenuity to its utmost.

Authors can also reveal personality by showing how setting enters into state of mind. We feel that after he eavesdrops on the celebrities in the restaurant, Basil has achieved a new peace, a sense of belonging in the world, because of the way he looks at it:

> It was dark outside and Broadway was a blazing forest fire as Basil walked slowly along toward the point of brightest light. He looked up at the great intersecting planes of radiance with a vague sense of approval and possession . . . .

Throughout *Twenty Thousand Leagues under the Sea* we know that for Aronnax outer Nature and his inner nature are married. He is most alive observing and interacting with the endless variety of marine phenomena: what the bird flying in the air looks like from under the water, how an underwater volcanic outpour looks when lack of air precludes flame, why sea-flowers have no "soul." Aronnax reveals himself as the happy Romanticist when he must record the very essence of each separate, unique phenomenon. For the characters in *Wuthering Heights*, their outdoor life so pervades their indoor life, their fireside speech is cast in metaphors drawn from nature:

> "Whatever our souls are made of," Catherine tells Nelly, "his [Heathcliff's] and mine are the same; and Linton's is as different as a moonbeam from lightning, or frost from fire."

Setting: Symbolism

No wonder then that selected features of the environment become symbolic not only for the characters but for the reader too. Catherine and Heathcliff live at Wuthering Heights, which is, as Lockwood has told us, rude, exposed to nature, a stormy, dynamic place. Linton lives at the Thrushcross Grange, situated in a well-protected, serene and peaceful valley, by comparison, a static place. The two natural settings come to symbolize two attitudes toward life, the passionate and the refined, as well as two levels of economic well-being, the difficult and the comfortable.

For Captain Nemo, and hence for us readers too, the sea symbolizes all the things he loves—freedom, mystery, and variety within unity, the ever new, flexible, and mobile.

Setting can become so symbolic for characters that it penetrates into their dreams and so gives us additional information about their personalities. Aronnax has been happy in his sheltered life on the submarine. One day he and his comrades go into a cave on an island, the submarine base, and take a nap. The tide changes and the cave is flooded. Later, Aronnax tells us he dreamed he was "a simple mollusk. This cave was now the shell that enclosed me in its bivalves." Verne reveals Aronnax's deepest, most unconscious longing — to withdraw from the world entirely — in terms of symbols translated from the immediate setting.

Setting: Themes

Ultimately, then, we see that setting also points to the themes of a work of fiction. In *Wuthering Heights*, the two main settings help us distinguish between the life of passion and the life of refinement and sobriety. Thus, they help us understand Brontë's main message: the need to achieve a balance between emotion and reason.

In Verne's novel, setting helps us understand the Romanticist beliefs that man must respect nature, even define himself through nature. In *The Jungle*, we find that Sinclair's careful documentation of the working-class environment in Chicago in 1904 supports his main themes: that certain milieus can degrade human beings and that a new social order must free them from such environments.

Setting: Methods

Authors can describe setting in two basic ways. Let us call them the *direct and static* as opposed to the *indirect and dynamic*.

Direct and Static Approach

Often an author will describe a scene in his own voice, from his godlike position as "author omniscient." Thus John Steinbeck opens "Flight":

> About fifteen miles below Monterey, on the wild coast, the Torres family had their farm, a few sloping acres above a cliff that dropped to the brown reefs and to the hissing white waters of the ocean. Behind the farm stone mountains stood up against the sky. The farm buildings huddled like little clinging aphids on the mountain skirts, crouched low to the ground as though the wind might blow them into the sea. The little shack, the rattling, rotting barn were gray-bitten with sea salt, beaten by the damp wind until they had taken on the color of the granite hills.

Indirect and Dynamic Approach

Usually an author prefers the more artistic method of letting us discover the setting as it is perceived by the characters themselves: Wuthering Heights as seen by Lockwood, Broadway as experienced by Basil, distant Chicago as smelled and heard by the approaching immigrants. This method has the advantage in that it integrates description into the action and immediately lets us gauge the effect of the milieu on personalities.

Evaluating Setting

You now have some criteria for judging an author's success in use of setting.

☆ Does he contrive artistic ways of "looking" at the environment?

☆ Does the milieu he creates help the reader suspend disbelief?

☆ Does the setting contribute to suspense? to mood? How?

☆ Does it help shape, test, and reveal character? How?

☆ Does setting take on significant symbolic value? Explain.

☆ How does setting help formulate the author's themes?

Point of View

Upton Sinclair is very audible as the storyteller. He narrates *The Jungle* himself, in his own voice. But Jules Verne is never heard from in *Twenty Thousand Leagues under the Sea*. Rather, he lets one of his characters, Professor Aronnax, tell us the story.

Why do authors sometimes monopolize, sometimes delegate, the powers of narrator? What are the advantages and disadvantages of each approach? How does each approach affect plot, characterization, setting, style, and themes? We consider these to be questions of *literary point of view*—that is, that point in human awareness from which action is observed and related.

You should note, incidentally, that in literary discussion, *point of view* means much more than "opinion" or "attitude," although these may be involved. If we say that Brontë tells her story from *Lockwood's point of view*, we have the larger meaning in mind. She tells the story as it registers on, as well as filters through, *Lockwood's ken*.

Author as Omniscient Narrator

The point of view that authors most commonly adopt is that of the *omniscient narrator*. The writer simply claims for himself all the godlike powers granted to the storyteller by time-honored tradition. He can stand far above his creation and give us an overall view or he can zoom in for a closeup. He can show us a character as he appears to others and then he can put us inside that character. Always, however, he maintains some distance by speaking of his characters in the third person: *she, he, they*. He can take us back and forth across time and space and show us how seemingly separate, unconnected events are really related. He knows the future of his characters and can give us as much foreknowledge of it as he wants. Indeed he can editorialize whenever he sees fit.

Sinclair uses this approach in *The Jungle,* as you must have realized by now. A more recent example would be Kurt Vonnegut's *Breakfast of Champions.*

You enjoy the *omniscient narrator* approach because it makes you the *omniscient reader.* You know more of the world in which the story is set than does any character in it. And so you can enjoy to the utmost what we call *dramatic irony.* This is a situation in which the audience, privy to information a character does not have, contemplates the way the character performs in his ignorance. In reading an author-omniscient story, you can especially enjoy that power of transcendency we have mentioned as one of literature's greatest appeals.

For some readers, the author-omniscient approach does have its shortcomings. The author makes us privy to so many lives, we get few of the benefits of immersing ourselves thoroughly in one life, as we would with other approaches. And the author's own presence can be an intrusion, influencing our own judgments, coming between us and the characters. Indeed, the author-omniscient often yields to the temptation to insert essays into the novel, giving us his/her own views of the character's predicament or even of larger social issues. For some modern readers, especially those who prefer a psychological emphasis in fiction, this is a further disruption of their concentration on the quality of the characterization.

But in the hands of a highly original writer like Vonnegut, the omniscient-narrator approach has enjoyed a popular comeback. It's a clear matter of relationship between theme and philosophy on the one hand and literary maneuver on the other. Vonnegut believes strongly that the reader must never be allowed to forget that the creation and the creator are aspects of each other. And he *wants* to emphasize his message, to point out the meaning of the action *to him.* His novel is *his* statement. Thus, in *Breakfast of Champions,* he uses certain scenes and his running commentary on them as an argument against the prevailing practice of dividing the *dramatis personae* into major and minor characters. Because he is able to make his little authorial intrusions amusing, he has demonstrated that the author-as-omniscient-narrator point of view still has its artistic value.

Author as Limited Narrator

An author can achieve different effects by changing his stance as narrator. First of all, he can still tell the story himself but focus mainly on one character, limiting his and our view to what that one person can know, do, and discover. The author still maintains his distance, still talking of people in the third person: *him, her, them.* Thus, the reader too is at least partly outside the character, enjoying now the author's observations, now the character's view. The main advantage is that the reader can more thoroughly identify with one person. Another advantage is that there is a kind of intensification of suspense: Limited as we are to what one person can perceive, limited as we are to his or her time and place, we are as ignorant as he/she is of much of what awaits him/her.

Our main example of author-narrator limited to a *main character* has been Fitzgerald's ''The Freshest Boy.'' A more extended example would be Wachtel's *Joe the Engineer.* Confined as we are by this approach to Joe's view of the world, we soon learn how horrible it is to have no advanced education and hence a job with monotonous routine and no future; to be surrounded by people who know more, and hence can understand more, than you do.

An author can gain different advantages by telling his story in his own voice, and in the third person, but from the point of view of a *minor character*. In other words, we see the main character as he/she affects an observer. In Joseph Conrad's "The Lagoon," a white man visits Arsat as his wife is dying. As they spend their night together in a deathbed vigil, Arsat tells his visitor about his life, especially about his relation with his brother. Thus, Arsat, the main character, is portrayed not only as he reveals himself but also as these revelations impress a visitor. And Conrad is able to illustrate one of his main themes. The absent brother comes to us only through the filter of Arsat's experience; Arsat comes to us through the filter of the white man's experience; and the white man is known to us only through the filter of the author's mind. Reality, life, Conrad is saying, is a series of impressions of impressions. And point of view, we see again, can definitely point toward theme.

Author as Objective Narrator

So far we have seen the author operating in situations where he *may* give us his own views but certainly *does* take us inside one or more characters to glean *their* views. He has one other point of view he can assume while still narrating in his own voice in the third person. He can refrain from saying anything directly to the reader *and* from going inside any character. A famous example of this approach is Ernest Hemingway's "The Killers."

Two gunmen enter a restaurant and force the employees and a customer to help set up an ambush for a boxer who usually comes there for dinner. The gunmen leave after the pugilist fails to show. One of the employees, Nick, goes to a rooming house to tell the boxer that mobsters are after him. Nick returns to the restaurant where he and his co-workers numbly, briefly remark on the situation.

We identify with no one in particular. We observe everyone *from the outside*. Everything is presented objectively, as though Hemingway had filmed the action and taped the conversation.

Again, point of view helps establish the author's themes. Through this externality of narration, Hemingway tells us: This is a society of grim, resigned, tight-lipped men; a cold, atomized society of people with a frozen, impenetrable inner life.

Character as Narrator

As we have suggested, the author may limit his own visibility even more drastically by dropping the storyteller role entirely and turning the narrator's job over to a character. The story is told now not in author's *third* but in the character's *first person*: *I*. The reader is now completely inside one person involved in the action, with all the advantages and disadvantages that implies.

The gap between us and the action is closed even further; we are more intimate with at least one personality. But we have less chance than ever of achieving overview. We can experience action and judge other characters only to the extent that the narrator is aware of them. We are limited to the perceptiveness of the mind whose *line of sight* we experience. How close we can get to the center of things depends on just who the narrator is: a *minor* character? a *main* character? the *hero/heroine*?

Minor Character as Narrator

Emily Brontë decides to reveal the vast complex drama of *Wuthering Heights* only as it yields to the curiosity of a character so minor we can only describe him as a nosy observer. But Lockwood is well *motivated* to seek out the story. Having rented Thrushcross Grange from Heathcliff, Lockwood goes to visit his landlord at Wuthering Heights and is astonished by the nature of the people there. Then, contracting a cold and confined to bed, he begs the housekeeper, Nelly, to explain these people and their circumstances.

She tells of the tragic love of Heathcliff and Catherine and of the second generation of Grange and Heights people. Her information comes from her own experience as a servant in both places, at one time or another, as well as what she has seen and been told in conversation and letters. Late in the novel, Lockwood, no longer a tenant, visits the Heights and himself pieces together the conclusion of the saga.

Obviously Brontë invented the techniques Conrad uses in "The Lagoon" (and oddly enough gets credit for as a major innovation in works like *Lord Jim*). That is, we comprehend an already complex human situation only as it filters through to us from several minds. Nelly is hardly a passive reporter; rather, she is an officious meddler in the lives of the people she "explains" to Lockwood. How much of the story has she distorted, unwittingly or tendentiously? And Lockwood is a cynical, worldly, urbane man fascinated by the intensity and grossness of country emotions. How much of the already distorted story has he *reflected*, how much *refracted*?

The reader is actively involved in trying to understand the main characters through all the help and hindrance provided by the minor characters. This form of subjective fiction actually induces the reader to participate in a dynamic psychological situation.

Major Character as Narrator

We get closer to the center of action, and we become more intimate with the narrator, if he/she is a main character, that is, describing not as an observer but as a participant. Our best example has been Verne's *Twenty Thousand Leagues under the Sea*. The hero is Captain Nemo, the person closest to Nemo is Aronnax, and Aronnax tells the story. Again the author has thoroughly *motivated* his narrator's curiosity; Aronnax has a great personal, professional, and public need to know the secrets of Nemo's life. He is less successful than Lockwood in getting the ultimate facts, but in his struggle, Aronnax gives us that extra advantage we have when the narrator is a main character: We experience more intensive intimacy with him. The *I* here is not the reporter's *I* but the lyrical *I*.

We know Lockwood's mind mainly as a means to an end of learning the story. We know Aronnax also as an end in himself, a round, complex character we enjoy being inside. And we experience again that special tension in reading first-person fiction: We have to make our own adjustments for what we can only guess are reflections and refractions of Nemo's character as it comes to us through Aronnax's ken.

Hero/Heroine as Narrator

The gap between the reader and the central character is closed entirely when the author lets the hero/heroine tell his/her own story as *I*. But here again we have less overview; our understanding is limited to what one mind can learn, and to the *order* in which it can learn the facts. The only objective information we can garner about the central character is what he/she wittingly or unwittingly reveals. On the other hand, we enjoy immersing ourselves entirely in a personality outside ourselves, learning all over again that reality is different to every person, and so immeasurably enriching the *vicarious* experience that we go to fiction for.

A good recent example of this approach is Barbara Girion's *A Tangle of Roots*. We learn from the inside of Beth the anguish of losing one's mother in one's adolescence; of having to rebuild one's whole world; of rediscovering one's own father as a changing person; of coming to terms with death, painfully and slowly, as a fact of life. And we gain again the peculiar benefit of first-person narration: We see how each mind, like Beth's, like Aronnax's, in effect recreates other people, like Beth's father, like Nemo, according to the original mind's needs.

Shifting Narrators

We have examined six different points of view authors can use. When they decide to tell the story in their own voice, they can be *omniscient* (outside and inside of everybody), or *limited* (inside certain characters only), or *objective* (outside of everybody). When they decide to let a character tell the story, they can choose among the advantages of using as the narrator a *minor character* (not close to the central action), a *main character* (closer), or the *hero/heroine* (the center).

The first three—*author as narrator*—tend to provide a more *objective view*. The last three—*character as narrator*—tend to provide a *subjective view* of reality.

But to these six points of view we can add many variations and combinations. Two examples will suffice to show how authors consider the way *shifting* the point of view will affect plot, characterization, and theme.

In *Lord Jim*, Conrad opens his story in the conventional manner. He is the author omniscient, able to take the reader to any place, into any time, in order to set his stage. But near the end of Chapter 4, as Jim is a witness at a court of inquiry, his eyes meet Captain Marlow's eyes. Abruptly, Marlow takes over the story. From Chapter 5 on, we hear about Lord Jim as Marlow prefers to tell the story at dinner parties.

Some of his impressions come from his personal contacts with Jim, as when that miserable young man relates how he realized he had actually abandoned his post. Many observations derive from Marlow's earlier discussions about Jim with other people. Some vital facts in the story Marlow has actually received third-hand!

This shift from *omniscient author as narrator* to *observer as narrator* reinforces two of Conrad's great strengths: his constant renewal of *suspense* and his *characterization* of any hero as a composite of impressions. Conrad believes that *esse est percipi*—to be is to be perceived—and so it is an author's job to reflect the hero as he has impressed himself on others.

An even more complex example of *shifting points of view* is William Faulkner's *As I Lay Dying*. As Addie Bundren lies dying, the author has sixteen characters reveal—each in the first person—his or her reaction. Each narrator emerges as a separate person, with his own secrets and emotional biases, yet the total effect is of a larger, overall *family consciousness*.

Evaluating Point of View

Thinking about an author's choice and use of point of view obviously provides you with a rich subject matter for and a fruitful approach to your book report writing.

☆ From which angle does the author prefer to witness the action?

☆ How does his point of view affect the order in which events are revealed—that is, the plot?

☆ What does point of view reveal about the characters (observing and observed)?

☆ How does it help us comprehend the theme?

Style and Tone

You will find that an author's *style* is that aspect of his/her work easiest to react to and hardest to explain. But if we first consider some ways the word *style* is commonly used, we can quickly narrow down its implications.

Style is the person is one expression we often hear. Whether the person is an actress, baseball player, violinist, or writer, we talk of his/her style to mean *overall approach*, the way that person characteristically functions. Applied to an author, then, style might include his/her typical *matter* as well as *manner*: story, message, themes, as well as structure, point of view, and texture of language.

Style is the right word in the right place is another common definition. Here the aim seems to be to concentrate on the author's *diction* (choice of words), *syntax* (arrangement of those words), and related factors like *metaphor*, *simile*, and *symbolism* (use of comparisons).

Attic style, Romanticist style, Byronic style are typical of many expressions we hear that try to characterize an author's individual style by relating it to the typical manner of a certain age or literary movement. Thus, an *Attic style* aims at the purity and simplicity of language and structure that the ancient Athenians admired. A *Zolaist style* would include not only the documentary, objective kind of reportage in the writing itself, the scientific manner advocated by Zola, but also the broad socioeconomic coverage of subject matter he called for.

Since we are considering an author's matter (story, themes) and certain aspects of manner (plot, point of view, setting) under separate headings, you can see that we mean here to use the word *style* in a narrow sense: the way an author gives *texture to language*, the way the *language gains tone*. In fiction writing, then, style can be broken down into an author's way with words, sentence maneuvers, dialogue, and use of evocative comparisons.

Style: A Way with Words

You enjoy reading an author who regularly pulls things together by using the right word in the right place. This often means that in the context of a series of *objective words*, he or she will place a pertinent *qualitative word*. When you chuckled over the little boy's sneering remark to Basil . . .

"Go on, hit me!" he chirped nervously.

. . . you were especially enjoying the word *chirped* which summed up the quality of the child's voice and his physical appearance. And notice how in the following passage Fitzgerald again sums up the *facts* with a word that gives us the *crux* of the facts:

"I don't like football. I don't like to go out and get a crack in the eye." Lewis spoke aggressively, for his mother had canonized all his timidities as common sense.

Fitzgerald has not only given us an example of Lewis' timidity, in his own words, but has summed up the *effect* of the mother's encouragement of timidity by using the word *canonized*: She has dignified his weaknesses by raising them to the level of church law! She has glorified, sanctioned, and exalted them! And Fitzgerald gets across these many connotations with *one word*!

In the two examples cited, the author has enhanced his characterization by finding a single word that points it up. Notice what the *crucial phrases* accomplish in these examples:

As Joe the Engineer, bored and morose, rides to work in a utilities company car, his fellow meter reader tries to cheer him up by citing the benefits of his having a job. The chapter ends with Joe's answer:

"It's a job."

In "The Killers," after Nick returns from warning the boxer and talks about it to his co-workers, the story ends:

"Well," said George, "you better not think about it."

In these last two examples, certain crucial phrases have been placed in *the crucial place*—the end of the chapter or story—so as to especially enhance the *mood* and point to the *theme*. If these "right" but rather ordinary expressions had been placed earlier, they would have lost their impact and much of their importance.

Fitzgerald, Wachtel, and Hemingway use *qualitative* and/or *crucial* words sparingly, and this contributes to their lean, functional style. Other authors, like Conrad, prefer a lush, velvety texture. In "The Lagoon" Conrad writes:

Nothing moved on the river but the eight paddles that rose flashing regularly, dipped together with a single splash, while the steersman swept right and left with a periodic and sudden flourish of his blade describing a glinting semicircle above his head.

Every word here has been selected for the way it advances the *action*, contributes to *color* or *setting*, and creates an overall impression of *human motion and commotion*. This of course also contributes to Conrad's *theme*, as we have noted it: the incredible complexity of the simplest experience.

One secret of the success of this passage is Conrad's emphasis on *action* words: three complete verbs (*moved, rose, swept*), four verb participles (*flashing, dipped, describing, glinting*), and two nouns that connote verbs (*splash, flourish*). Another secret is Conrad's selection of words that set up sound patterns, a *sibilance* in the succession of fla*sh*ing, *s*pla*sh*, *s*teer*s*man, *s*wept, *s*udden flouri*sh*, de*s*cribing, *s*emicircle, and a *clatter* in pa*ddl*es, fla*sh*ing, spla*sh*.

Conrad even goes so far as to use the hunt for the right word as the *verbal equivalent* of his probing into character and the nature of reality. Wanting to equate Romantic love with *imbecility*, Marlow feels he must focus better:

> "... the imbecility, not a repulsive imbecility, the exalted imbecility of these proceedings ..."

Even physical description becomes a series of revisions for him. "A faint noise of thunder" is refocused:

> "... of thunder infinitely remote, less than a sound, hardly more than a vibration ..."

Style: Sentence Maneuvers

One way, then, that the prose artist achieves an appropriate style is to enhance his *factual words* with a goodly proportion of *qualitative words*. Another way is judiciously to vary the structure and even the length of his sentences. As Basil Lee and Lewis Crum sit facing each other on the train, Fitzgerald compares them not only with the words he uses but also by the way he balances his terms:

> Lewis
> > the veteran
> > > was miserable
>
> Basil
> > the neophyte
> > > was happy
>
> Lewis
> > plunged deeper
> > > into misery and homesickness
>
> Basil
> > had a glad feeling
> > > of recognition and familiarity

This *parallel structure* is the inevitable form for Fitzgerald's message.

For a study of judicious use of sentence patterns, we can do no better than to consult the fiction of James Agee, a master of prose form. See how in "A Mother's Tale" he uses *parallelism* to supply the contours for his picture of how a herd of cattle moves:

> Those in front were compelled by those behind; those at the rear ... did their best to keep up; those who were locked within the herd could no more help moving than the particles inside a falling rock.

Agee achieves some of his best effects by a judicious mixture of *loose sentences* and *periodic sentences*. In a *loose sentence*, the main idea is expressed first and then it is qualified:

> They were at a walk, not very fast, but faster than they could imaginably enjoy.

In a *periodic sentence*, the main idea is deliberately held for last, with many postponements that build suspense:

> They were fed and watered so generously, and treated so well, and the majesty and loveliness of this place where they had all come to rest was so far beyond anything they had ever known or dreamed of, that many of the simple and ignorant, whose memories were short, began to wonder whether that whole difficult journey, or even their whole lives up to now, had ever really been.

As he mixes *sentence structures*, so the artistic writer mixes *sentence lengths*. Agee will vary from a rolling, cumulative 70-word sentence like the one above to a quick, simple six-word statement:

> Other spring calves came galloping too.

The fiction writer varies the length of his sentences to pace the movement of their meaning. Thus Fitzgerald writes of the headmaster's puzzlement over Basil's predicament:

> Among boys and masters there seemed to exist an extraordinary hostility toward him, and though Doctor Bacon had dealt with many sorts of schoolboy crimes, he had neither by himself nor with the aid of trusted sixth-formers been able to lay his hands on its underlying cause. It was probably no single thing, but a combination of things; it was most probably one of those intangible questions of personality. Yet he remembered that when he first saw Basil he had considered him unusually prepossessing. He sighed.

Going from a 47-word sentence to a 22-worder to a 15-worder to a two-worder, Fitzgerald gradually contracts Bacon's thinking into a single sound.

Style: Dialogue

The style of the fiction writer, like that of the playwright, must be judged largely in terms of dialogue. The first essential consideration is that the author's own voice, in his narration and description, sound different from his character's voices. Please read the 47-word sentence again, beginning "Among boys and masters . . ." Now read:

> "You get up to New York only once a month," Lewis Crum was saying, "and there you have to take a master along."
>
> "I'd just duck the master when I got to New York," said Basil.
>
> "Yes, you would."
>
> "I bet I would."
>
> "You try it and you'll see."
>
> "What do you mean saying I'll see, all the time, Lewis? What'll I see?"

Fitzgerald's "Among boys" passage is composed with the deliberate logic and rhythm of sustained expository prose. The boys' sentences are composed to reflect the structure and music of short, spontaneous, alternating speeches. An author considers it so important to make these two modes sound different that Hemingway used to compose narrative at the typewriter, sitting at his coffee table, and dialogue in long hand, standing at the mantlepiece! Thus, going from a posture of observation to a stance of participation, he kept himself reminded of the need to change pace.

The second consideration, of course, is that each character have his/her own characteristic speech. Notice how Emily Brontë makes these two men sound different, starting on the very first page:

"Mr. Heathcliff?" I said.

A nod was the answer.

"Mr. Lockwood, your new tenant, sir. I do myself the honour of calling as soon as possible after my arrival, to express the hope that I have not inconvenienced you in my perseverance in soliciting the occupation of Thrushcross Grange; I heard yesterday you had had some thoughts—"

"Thrushcross Grange is my own, sir," he interrupted, wincing. "I should not allow anyone to inconvenience me, if I could hinder it—walk in!"

These characters differ in their *diction*, their *syntax*, their *sentence rhythms*. Later Brontë will characterize Catherine by her highly imaginative use of *evocative comparisons*. She tells Nelly:

"My love for Linton is like the foliage in the woods: time will change it . . . as winter changes the trees. My love for Heathcliff resembles the eternal rocks beneath—a source of little visible delight, but necessary."

In other words, just as authors themselves manifest their individual style in their unique blends of diction, syntax, and imagery, so should their characters.

Style: Evocative Comparisons

Catherine explains what Nelly does not know—the nature of her two loves—in terms of what Nelly does know—the relative permanence of foliage and rocks. Earlier we read Agee's explanation that those animals ". . . who were locked within the herd could no more help moving than the particles inside a falling rock."

His figure of speech invites us to judge the new, unfamiliar phenomenon (cows in a moving herd) in terms of the old, familiar concepts (atoms whirling inside a "solid" structure in motion). Such *metaphors* shock us by forcing us to assimilate a *similarity between dissimilars*. The shock makes the event an emotional one and aids us in achieving vicarious experience of the characters' emotional states. In reading *Slaughterhouse-Five*, we sharply comprehend a dying colonel's breathing because Vonnegut likens it to something we know but did not expect to hear in this context:

Every time he inhaled his lungs rattled like greasy paper bags.

We understand the position, the crowdedness of prisoners sleeping on a floor because they "nestled like spoons."

Such evocative comparisons keep our imagination fired up, make us participants in the story, create a special kind of suspense for the author's next use of metaphor.

Metaphor likens unlike things. The most powerful and compact of all metaphors is the *symbol*. A symbol is something that stands for something else, but something larger than itself; often it is a *material* thing or a *specific* action that represents something *immaterial* or *general*.

We have already seen how two settings—Wuthering Heights and Thrushcross Grange—come to symbolize two different modes of existence. When Jurgis flees to the country, he bathes in a stream and washes away his old life: Sinclair clearly intends us to see Jurgis as being baptized anew. Later when Jurgis pulls up trees newly planted by a mean farmer, we feel it is a symbolic rehearsal for a rebellion. Sinclair also uses time for ironic symbolism: Ona's two fateful absences from home occur just before Thanksgiving and Christmas.

When an author *sustains* a symbolic action so that the surface story conceals a more covert story, we call it *allegory*. Sinclair's famous allegory in *The Jungle* implies a parallel between hogs and human beings.

> Each one of these hogs was a separate creature. Some were white hogs, some were black. . . . And each of them had an individuality of his own, a will of his own. . . . each was full of self-confidence, of self-importance, and a sense of dignity. And trusting and strong in faith he had gone about his business, the while a black shadow hung over him and a horrid Fate waited in his pathway. Now suddenly it had swooped upon him, and had seized him by the leg. . . . it cut his throat and watched him gasp out his life. . . . Jurgis . . . turned to go . . . and muttered: "*Dieve*—but I'm glad I'm not a hog."

Later, when Jurgis realizes that the packers have used him just as they use hogs, the allegory, one story overlaid on another, is completed. And when the meaning of the allegory becomes clear, it becomes part of the overall theme.

Style and Tone

Style is a major component of what we perceive as the *tone* of a work, that is, the attitude of the writer. It corresponds to *tone of voice* in speech. When someone answers you by saying "Yes," you have to infer his full meaning by the tone of his voice. For "Yes" can actually mean "Yes, but . . ." or "Really, is that so?" or "Absolutely!" or "What do you want?" or "What are you getting at?"

In his writing, an author must add such overtones and undertones with literary emphases, such as we have been considering here as stylistic maneuvers. Even so, a reader may miss the full implications of an author's *tone*, just as a listener may fail to get the subtle inflections added to a spoken statement. You have largely to use your own intuition when you decide how to describe an author's tone.

His attitude will be easier to characterize if he is himself acting as narrator. Thus, it's clear that Sinclair is himself now indignant, now sarcastic, now sentimental over the fate of his people. Fitzgerald is concerned, understanding, sympathetic toward human weakness but also firm in his belief that it must be overcome. Hemingway's attitude *seems* to be impartial, reportorial, letting circumstances speak for themselves (but of course they speak for him too because he arranged them to give the impression that they do).

The author's own attitude is harder to describe if he/she lets a character tell the story. The tone of *Wuthering Heights* is more urbane, sophisticated, and faintly cynical when Lockwood is reporting his own impressions. The tone becomes more judgmental, more severe, when Nelly is controlling the narration. But when we remind ourselves that it's Brontë herself who represents all points of view, even Lockwood's, we can only say that the author's own attitude is one of profound compassion for all variations of the human condition. Her final attitude must be inferred from her overall message.

With Conrad—whether he tells his own story, as in "The Lagoon," or lets Marlow tell it, as in *Lord Jim*—we sense a prevailing tone of infinite but unfulfilled curiosity in the face of impenetrable mystery. Conrad's attitude seems to be that the more he understands, the less he can judge. In his case, *tone* points toward message, *theme*.

Evaluating Style

You can prepare yourself for discussing an author's style by first asking yourself general questions like these:

☆ Have I been—consciously or unconsciously—captured and carried along by the language? Or have I had trouble getting into the book and staying with it?

Yes or no, you should get on to specific questions which will help you understand why you've been attracted or repelled, questions like:

☆ Does the author have "a way with words" that puts his/her facts in focus?

☆ Are the author's sentences cast in a form that reinforces their content? Do his/her sentence structure, length, and rhythm vary according to the unfolding action?

☆ Does each character speak in patterns that differ from those of other characters and of the author?

☆ Has the author heightened my insight, stirred my imagination, exalted my feelings through an appropriate use of metaphor and symbol?

☆ How has the *tone* of the language influenced my reactions? Whom does the tone represent, character or author?

☆ How have style and tone indicated theme?

Pondering such questions will help you decide what, *in your opinion*, are the strengths and weaknesses of the author's style. Of course, make note of good examples of each strength, each weakness.

Final Statement of Theme

You have probably noticed, as we examined one by one the components of fiction, that:

1. Each component—plot, characterization, setting, point of view, style, tone—has usually been designed to contribute to the *theme(s)*.

2. By *theme*, we seem to mean, at various times, *subject, central idea, thesis, message, lesson, moral, overall meaning*.

3. Indeed, when we try to state all the *conclusions* we can derive from a story, we realize that, like a piece of music, a work of fiction comprises both *themes* and *motifs*. (A motif is a part of a theme, a subtheme.)

4. Finally, some messages, some conclusions, are made *explicit* in the story, while others are only *implied*. The sensitive, careful, trained reader realizes then that some of the themes will occur to him/her only as she/he reflects on the reading experience.

You are ready then to pull together, from all the explicit and implied messages, a full statement of the overall significance of a work of fiction. For example:

Themes: *The Jungle*

Looking back over Sinclair's novel, you are reminded that he deliberately writes on two levels, shifting continually from one to the other. Now he dramatizes his subject matter, letting it speak for itself; now he interprets it, not only summing up its social significance, but also giving his own conclusions and opinions. So many of Sinclair's conclusions are so thoroughly indicated by settings, situations, moods, metaphors, and symbols that you could have derived them for yourself, without the author's reformulations. But some of Sinclair's conclusions may seem personal and many readers might disagree.

Your treatment of his themes, then, would involve you in a discussion of which of these *explicit* conclusions are actually *implicit* in the novel proper, and which are imposed? You might want to start with a list of *stated themes* and *motifs*, such as:

★ In 1900–1904, Big Business has complete control of—but no responsibility for—the well-being of American workers.

★ Workers are brutalized and stultified. Only that part of their personality needed to perform their monotonous tasks is kept alive. The rest is crushed. Under such conditions, love is reduced to bestiality, the human aspects of marriage and child-raising are overshadowed by economic agonies, and love and marriage have become economic traps.

★ Equality of opportunity is a myth. Capitalist democracy is therefore a contradiction.

★ The only solution is to transfer industry from private to public control through democratic procedures.

Now you would want to check back and see which of these explicit conclusions can be justified in the story itself.

Themes: "The Freshest Boy"

You of course could start from Basil's explicit remarks to himself about what he has learned: Life is a struggle for everyone and (look at Broadway!) the struggle is worth it. But with a little reflection, you can see other messages *implied* in the situation. Basil has made such observations and resolutions before; the difference, the change, is that now he understands that insight must prove itself in action. And how he got the insight is a message in itself: He was able to profit from the experiences of others and to read signals in the environment. To put it another way, Fitzgerald has dramatized the difference between childhood and adulthood and how one makes the transition.

Themes: "The Killers"

Contemplating the meaning of Hemingway's story, you would find that nothing is made explicit by either author or character. From the way the characters act and talk, you realize that Hemingway is *indicating* that the world is in the grip of raw power, evil power. And the way he implicitly contrasts the restaurant workers' reactions allows you yourself to note crucial differences in character. Sam and George, numbed by false worldliness and lack of courage, do not want to be involved. Only young Nick is still innocent enough to be shocked. Hemingway, you might infer, is saying that we must take a stand on evil before we become numbed by its prevalence.

But a careful rereading of the text gives you some subtle insights. Sam and George work in Henry's lunchroom; Mrs. Bell runs Mrs. Hirsch's rooming house; the gangsters are killing not for their own reasons but for their employers'. Hemingway portrays a world in which, he seems to say, no one has any personal stake in what he is doing. Indeed, no one seems to have any close friend. How are these factors related to the general numbness, the lack of involvement?

Fitzgerald and Hemingway have given you all the materials you need, but they require that you establish much of their meaning for yourself. This will always be your ultimate joy in reading fiction: the connections you must make, the way you must participate in order to complete the experience.

Themes: Universal Value Questions

All writers—whether they work in fiction, drama, or poetry—tend to return to the same great universal questions. You will find six of these universal value questions listed in the chapter on drama under the heading "Theme and Total Effect," page 85.

Chapter 3

How to Analyze and Evaluate Drama

HOW TO ANALYZE AND EVALUATE DRAMA

As you prepare to write a book report about a play, you face many problems similar to those you have faced with fiction, but you also take on new problems that are peculiar to drama.

Reading a play, you once again are concerned with *how and why characters change and what their situation tells us about the human condition*. And again you are alert to the *techniques* the author employs both to achieve his effects and to focus our experience on his *theme*.

Essential Differences

But you will write a better book report if you also keep in mind how the playwright's techniques differ from the novelist's.

First of all, the dramatist does not intend that you *read* what he has written (as does the novelist) but that you *watch* how actors and stage technicians stage his conceptions. So, if you happen to be *reading* a play as literature, instead of *sensing* it as drama, you must yourself supply some of the dramatic elements by a judicious use of imagination. You have to read stage directions and descriptions of settings as carefully as you read dialogue, appreciating to the fullest the role of spectacle as well as the role of language. For example, suppose a spirited dialogue between two lovers is interrupted by this simple stage direction:

[*They pause and stare searchingly at each other*]

You must avoid the temptation to go on reading and instead approximate your conduct in the theater. There, when

[*They pause and stare searchingly at each other*]

you too would be pausing, wondering why they are, and what their *unspoken reactions* might be. Again, when you read Act II of *Waiting for Godot* and you find Beckett saying

The tree has four or five leaves

you have carefully to visualize the scene, recall that in Act I there were *no* leaves, and consider the significance of the change in spectacle.

Secondly, you have to keep in mind the difference in point of view. In fiction, Upton Sinclair can put himself *inside* the action, commenting on it. Or, Emily Brontë can have *her* story narrated by one of the characters, told therefore from *his* point of view. Or, Ernest Hemingway can put himself *outside* the action to the extent that we know a character's internal experience only as he himself reveals it.

The modern dramatist usually has no such range of options. By the very nature of the medium, the playwright can work only objectively, somewhat like Hemingway, always staying outside the action, outside the characters' minds. Indeed, once our experience of a work is underway, we are less aware of the playwright's presence than we are of any fiction writer's, less even than of Hemingway's. In short, in fiction the writer may or may not be present, but in drama the writer is absent.

There are at least three important results of this invisibility of the writer of drama: (1) The audience—spectators or readers—is brought closer to the action and can observe without interference, unaware of the writer as intermediary. (2) The audience can more easily achieve "willing suspension of disbelief," since they are not forced to translate printed page into action but can observe it directly. And (3) the playwright has to convert all his material into action, for there is no interesting way for him to put it into essay form, to offer it as his own commentary.

This emphasis on *conflict* and *spectacle* then, rather than on overt presentation of *ideas*, means that the drama audience may have a greater responsibility to *infer* ideas than does the fiction reader.

Finally, you should keep in mind that the dramatist's special aims and techniques have given rise to a special technical vocabulary. You can better understand your own reactions to drama, and make your book reports better understood, if you use this special terminology whenever appropriate.

Some More Specialized Knowledge

Types of Drama

In several times and places — especially in classical Greece and Rome, Elizabethan England, and neoclassicist France—drama has been rigidly divided into tragedy and comedy. *Tragedy* is that form of drama in which the hero or heroine, a person of superior mind, character, and social position, is overcome by the major problems he or she tackles. *Comedy*, on the contrary, involves common people who face lesser, often everyday, problems and succeed. Simplistically put, tragedy leads to a catastrophic defeat, comedy to a happy ending. Tragedy both engages the deep emotions and studies themes of high-seriousness, while comedy strives mainly to entertain, often through the ridicule of characters, customs, or the absurdity of life itself.

When certain elements of comedy and tragedy are blended, the resulting drama may be called a *tragicomedy*. For example, serious action that could lead to a catastrophe may unexpectedly be resolved in a happy ending. Thus Shakespeare's so-called "bitter comedies"—like *Measure for Measure*—are often called tragicomedies.

In modern times, when almost all plays, however serious, include a realistic balance of the comic and the tragic, the playwright is very likely to call a stageplay simply a *drama*.

Terms for Characterization

Traditionally, the *tragic hero* suffers defeat because some weakness of character makes him/her unable to cope decisively with the extraordinary circumstances into which he/she is plunged. In Greek, this frailty was called *hamartia*, usually translated as *tragic flaw*. The downfall of Greek heroes is often brought about by *hubris*, or excessive self-confidence. Shakespeare's Hamlet is unable to avenge his father's death partly because of an indecisiveness so profound he cannot begin to comprehend it.

In plays where there is one outstanding, most important character, that character is called the *protagonist*. If there is one major character in strong opposition to the protagonist, that character is the *antagonist*. Thus, in Shakespeare's tragedy *Othello*, the character who deceives the *protagonist*, Othello, into doubting his wife's fidelity is the *antagonist*, Iago.

In modern plays, there very often will not be one single leading character; and when there is, as in G.B. Shaw's *Candida*, there is very likely to be no antagonist in the final sense of the term, i.e., no main *opponent* to the protagonist.

Indeed, in discussing modern drama, we are likely to drop the term *hero* altogether, perhaps even to substitute the term *anti-hero*. The reason is simply that the character in the modern play often finds that commitment to high, heroic ideals is impossible because he feels helpless in a world without values, a world over which he has no control. Willy Loman (note the implication of the name!) may be the leading character in Arthur Miller's *Death of a Salesman*, but you would be making a serious error in calling him the *hero*. You would get closer to the message of the play if you used the term *anti-hero*.

Catharsis

The most famous, perhaps too the most controversial, term used in discussion of drama is *catharsis* (purgation, cleansing). Aristotle used it as the climactic term in his famous definition of tragedy:

> A tragedy . . . is an imitation of an action that is serious . . . and in language with pleasurable accessories . . . in a dramatic, not a narrative form; with incidents arousing pity and fear, wherewith to accomplish its catharsis of such emotions.

Let us assume that Aristotle meant that when a tragedy excites its audience, it also drains off repressed emotions and so purifies them.

One controversy about *catharsis* is whether the dramatist *should* be "draining off" in the theater emotions that perhaps should be discharged elsewhere, for example, in social action against repression. Does the theatergoer, dissatisfied with his life circumstances, experience such *catharsis* (relief) in the theater that he lapses into passive acceptance? Many modern dramatists, like Henrik Ibsen, so structure their works that emotions are aroused but *not* purged in the theater. In *A Doll's House*, Ibsen tries to trigger strong feelings about the status of women that perhaps the conscientious theatergoer can resolve only in political action outside the theater.

You can consider *catharsis* in a very simple way when you write a book report about a play. Have you, after experiencing the tragedy of Othello or Willy Loman, *accepted* it as inevitable? If so, then Shakespeare and Miller have successfully aroused in you *emotional sympathy* for their character's fate, but then tempered it with intellectual understanding and relief. On the other hand, if you experience no *catharsis* in a play like *Waiting for Godot*, what might that say about Beckett's intentions? his themes?

Less controversial than Aristotle's concept of *catharsis* is his identification of the "formative elements" of drama. Adapting his terms to modern needs, we can identify them as *plot*, *character*, *language*, *spectacle*, and *theme and total effect*.

Plot

You will recall that we have already described *plot*, in our analysis of fiction, as an author's arrangement of the events of his story. He devises a series of incidents that (1) put his characters into conflict, (2) lead them to change either themselves or their life situation, or both, and (3) lead them and us to a greater understanding of the human condition. The plot makes clear what the characters' life is like *before*, *during*, and *after* this major change.

The dramatist uses a similar scheme to test his characters but with this difference: Having his audience's attention for only a few hours at most, he must be more economical, more compact in his presentation of material. He must be more selective, using fewer scenes, fewer settings, fewer situations, and even fewer characters than the novelist may employ.

Two Types of Plot

As you consider the function of plot in any specific play, you will find it helps to think in terms of two broad types of plot. A playwright may cast his materials into the *traditional plot structure*, one developed in ancient Greece and widely used in modern drama from Shakespeare to Neil Simon. You will find it easy to identify the traditional plot if you study its components as they are discussed here. However, many modern dramatists, like Anton Chekhov or Samuel Beckett, may well invent, for each play they write, a new *nontraditional structure* that better suits their needs in presenting character and message. This will be harder for you to describe but more rewarding to discuss.

Traditional Plot Structure

The conventional plot is usually characterized, first of all, by its reliance on *sharp conflict*. You will find that you can identify *outer conflict*, between characters, between groups, between ideologies, and *inner conflict*, between a character and her/himself. Let us see how conflict becomes obvious even as we just summarize the basic dramatic situation in several plays using traditional structure.

Conflict in a Light Comedy

Monsieur Pasquinot and Monsieur Bergamin, neighbors, have professed mortal enmity for each other's families. They have made their children promise never to have anything to do with their father's enemies. But Sylvette Pasquinot and Percinet Bergamin have fallen in love and plan to elope tonight at eight. That is the situation in *The Romancers*, a romantic comedy by Edmond Rostand, produced in France in 1894. In an English musical-comedy version, *The Fantasticks*, it is now enjoying a record run in Greenwich Village.

Conflict in a Shakespearean Tragedy

Othello, a Moorish general in the service of Venice, has eloped with Desdemona, daughter of a Venetian noble. Iago, one of Othello's officers, is furious that Othello has chosen Cassio to be his second in command. Iago decides to get his revenge on both superior officers by leading Othello to believe that Cassio and Desdemona are lovers. Iago has, as his accomplice, Roderigo, a spurned suitor of Desdemona. This is the situation in the first act of Shakespeare's *Othello* (1604?), a classic of world theater.

Conflict in a Greek Tragedy

Polynices has led an army against his brother Eteocles who has reneged on a promise to share the kingship of Thebes. After both brothers are killed in single combat, their uncle Creon, the new ruler, decrees that Eteocles should be buried with full honors but Polynices must be left unburied. The penalty for disobeying this decree is death. Antigone, sister of the dead brothers, decides she must bury Polynices as a religious and family duty: the gods' laws supersede manmade laws. So Sophocles opens his tragedy *Antigone* (440 B.C.), a perennial favorite in the theater.

Conflict in a TV Play

An old widow is determined to get a job so she can continue to pay her rent. Her daughter Annie is determined that Mother will retire and come live with Annie's family. Husband George admires his mother-in-law's attitude. His sister-in-law believes Annie sacrifices herself in vain efforts to gain her mother's love and is unwittingly trying to deprive the old lady of her independence. These are the initial circumstances in Paddy Chayefsky's classic TV drama from the Fifties (the "Golden Age of Television"), *The Mother.*

Analyzing Traditional Plot

You have your main evidence that a playwright is using traditional plot if *the conflict intensifies and builds up to a climax, followed by a loosening of the tension, a resolution.* In his famous critical work, *The Technique of Drama* (1863), the German playwright Gustav Freytag illustrated this pattern with a diagram now known as Freytag's Pyramid. We can adapt it to our needs:

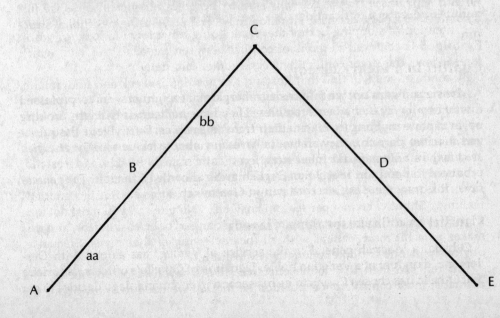

So Freytag charts the progress of a play from the Introduction or *Exposition* (A) to the *Rising Action* (B) culminating in the *Climax* (C); the *Falling Action* (D) leads to the Catastrophe or *Denouement* (E). That point or period in the Introduction when the main conflict is definitely triggered, Freytag calls "das irregende Moment" or the Initial or *Exciting Moment* (aa). The event that definitely indicates the turning point, and hastens the rising action toward the Climax is called the *Crisis* (bb). Let us study these terms as they relate to our examples.

Exposition

We think of the opening scenes as exposition because here the playwright has the difficult task of *explaining* the background situation and *introducing* his characters; he must do all this without holding up the action! Now *explanations* and *introductions* tend to be static, hence boring. The word *drama* means, literally, *action*. If characters pause to tell each other their life story, the result will be inaction and the audience will start yawning. Your first question, then, in judging the success of a play is this: Does the author get up momentum without unnecessary delay?

Sophocles swiftly sketches in the background situation for us by staging, as his opening scene, a surreptitious talk between Antigone and her sister, Ismene. We learn quickly where we are (in Thebes) and all about the recent battle, the brothers' deaths, and Creon's decree. The talk quickly flares into argument. Antigone intends to flout the decree and do her duty to the dead. But Ismene, speaking as Creon's subject, will obey him, and as a woman, will yield to men. The scene ends with Antigone contemptuous of her sister's timidity, Ismene nevertheless protesting her love.

A masterful exposition! In one short scene, Sophocles not only orients us in time and place, he introduces his main character, his theme (family loyalty versus loyalty to the state), and antagonisms between personalities and the sexes as well as between ideologies. Two of his characters are already contrasted and both off balance—the very stuff of drama.

Chayefsky reveals the background of *The Mother* by screening an early-morning argument in the bedroom of Annie and George. The husband querulously wants to know why the alarm has gone off at 6:30 A.M. In the next few minutes we learn significant details about the family history. The wife declares her intention of stopping her mother from going downtown to look for work. Exposition is achieved in terms of conflict between husband and wife which foreshadows the larger conflict between mother and daughter.

By contrast, you will find that Rostand's exposition is weak and undramatic. As the curtain goes up, we find ourselves looking at a garden—no, two gardens divided by a wall. On a bench on one side of the wall stands Sylvette, looking up in rapture as Percinet reads aloud from *Romeo and Juliet*. From their conversation we learn that they are not only *reading* about star-crossed lovers, they are *living* in a Romeo-and-Juliet situation.

But they spend too much time recalling the growth of their love. Rostand saves his draggy exposition by having Sylvette say, at one point in Percinet's reading, "Shhh!" Percinet pauses and answers, "No one . . . you must not take fright." We learn, then, that they are in some danger, or at least in fear, and this makes us a bit more patient with all the reviewing of their lives. Suspense, obviously, is one antidote to lengthy exposition.

You can see then that to be effective, like Chayefsky or Sophocles, the dramatist must contrive his exposition so that all we need to know about the *past* is unfolded while the conflicts develop in the *present* and some suspense is created about the *future*.

The Initial Moment

You will greatly enhance your understanding of dramatic structure—and be better able to discuss it in your book report—if you can identify the initial moment. This is an early dramatic event that greatly accelerates the rising action and shows conclusively that the hero is committed to trouble.

Continuing your study of *The Romancers*, for example, wouldn't you be able to sense the "moment" when it comes? The young lovers are dreaming aloud of fantastic solutions: Maybe there's a chance that Percinet might rescue Sylvette from kidnappers and then the fathers might relent and let the children marry. But they hear someone coming. They kiss and agree to meet at eight. Sylvette hides on her side of the wall. Percinet's father enters the garden, berates his son for his romantic love of fresh air, garden, and books, and announces he has arranged to marry Percinet to a rich woman. Percinet rejects the idea of "a marriage of reason," swears to marry only for love, and runs out of the garden. You *feel* the initial moment, of course, because the main conflict, only threatened until now, has been joined.

With *Othello* too you would probably have no trouble locating the exact moment when the action moves into high gear. After the main characters have been introduced and we have learned of Othello's exploits as a wooer and warrior, Iago soliloquizes on his plan for getting rid of Cassio which is

> . . . to abuse Othello's ear
> That he is too familiar with his wife.
> * * *
> I have't! It is engend'red! Hell and night
> Must bring this monstrous birth to the world's light.

From the very language, and from the fact that the speech comes at the end of the act, as the culmination of Iago's search for a means of revenge, you would realize that the main conflict has now been triggered.

Suppose you had difficulty finding an exact moment that can be said to accelerate the action. This would be true of *The Mother*. You would then be free to say of the playwright, as can be said here of Chayefsky, that the seam between exposition and rising action is impossible to find: they more than overlap, they are interwoven.

Dramatic Irony

Notice that we now know Iago's plan, but Othello, Desdemona, and Iago's wife, Emilia, do not. Shakespeare has added the element of dramatic irony, an artistic variation on literature's constant concern with the difference between appearance and reality. We shall watch how Othello and the two women will function in almost total ignorance of what is really going on. This private knowledge, this secret power that we have adds to that feeling of transcendence over circumstances that we can enjoy in fiction and drama. Again, vicarious experience adds to our knowledge of our own direct, real-life experience. For in real life we all function most of the time in at least partial ignorance of what other people know about us. Dramatic irony keeps us in awe of our terrible limitations.

Rising Action

The other names we can use for the rising action help us understand its nature: You may refer to it also as *the development* or *the complication* of the conflict. The hero or heroine's situation worsens; the antagonist looms as an even greater threat; suspense heightens.

Percinet's values are under attack; communication between him and his father has broken down; his future with Sylvette is imperiled. Now Rostand uses one of the most reliable devices in plot construction: *alternation of situations*, a device especially available to him because of his ingeniously divided stage. Alternation provides *balance, parallel action*, as we switch now to the other garden, other father, other lover. There Monsieur Pasquinot enters, berates his child too, and sends her off to take a note to a certain Monsieur Straforel. Rostand has made this second parent-child encounter a briefer one, for *variation* and *change of pace* are just as valuable as *alternation*.

Then, to our astonishment, Monsieur Pasquinot climbs over the wall and embraces his "enemy," Percinet's father! From their conversation we learn that the two fathers have actually hoped that their children would marry, but they have hesitated to tell the children that, because a marriage arranged by parents is "not as tempting" to young people as romantic as Percinet and Sylvette! Rather, the fathers have pretended to be feuding so that the children would be drawn closer by the sweet prospect of forbidden love!

Bergamin, we now learn, has eavesdropped on the lovers. He knows not only about their plans for eight o'clock, but also about their fantasies of a dramatic rescue. Hence the note to Straforel! It is his business—his and his six henchmen —to stage a kidnapping to give young heroes a chance to prove their mettle. Overjoyed at the thought of the romantic union of their families (not to mention their properties), the fathers embrace. But when Percinet and Sylvette enter, from their respective sides, the parents change their hug from one of affection to —physical combat!

Rostand has now made use of three further techniques. The confrontation between the fathers is a *dramatic reversal*: what happens is the exact opposite of what we have been led to expect. And their Straforel project is an *intrigue*. Again, as with Iago's project, we will experience *dramatic irony*. We will watch how Sylvette and Percinet act in their ignorance. We have been made privy to plans for a faked kidnapping, an abduction the lovers will think is real. *Suspense* is mounting and manifold. Will the lovers realize they are being duped? Will somebody get hurt? Worst of all, suppose Percinet is *not* willing to fight with six abductors?

Sophocles develops his rising action by a series of *confrontations* between Creon and five other characters. In the first, a guard reluctantly shambles onto stage to give Creon the unwelcome news: Someone has performed the ritual burial of Polynices. Furiously angry, Creon orders the sentry to uncover the body and find the person guilty. Next Creon faces Antigone, hears her defense, and sentences her to death. In this scene he also confronts Ismene, who reminds him that Antigone is engaged to marry his son, Haemon. Then Creon faces his son who cautions him: The people sympathize with Antigone and her ideas. Creon angrily declares that he cannot be swayed by the people; Haemon calls that folly. The tyrant decides to punish his son by having Antigone killed as Haemon watches. The son threatens vengeance and leaves. Finally Creon confronts Tiresias, the prophet, who warns the tyrant that the gods are displeased with his flouting of religious law about treatment of the dead. After his characteristic resort to anger, Creon now uncharacteristically sees he must be wrong and decides to undo the damage he has done.

Crisis to Climax

Rostand's comedy and Sophocles' tragedy, in other words, have reached the crisis, that is, the irreversible beginning of the climactic action. The crisis is that turning point after which things will never be the same again.

Rostand intensifies the critical situation by staging a *dramatic contrast*. In one garden, Straforel is placing his armed abductors. In the other, Percinet is waiting for the clock to strike eight. The playwright has alternated the mood: The gentle romantic vista is the calm before the storm we know is soon to burst upon us.

When Sylvette appears and is seized by the abductors, several of our anxieties are resolved. Percinet does *not* flee, he attacks and routs the swordsmen, and Straforel stages a minimal, token duel with Percinet and feigns a mortal wound. In a comedy, *climax* means the hero and heroine triumph.

In Sophocles' play, however, Creon's change of mind has come too late to give Antigone the victory she deserves. To meet Tiresias' demands, Creon must first order a tomb built for Polynices. Then he can go to release Antigone from her prison. But there he finds Antigone has hanged herself. Haemon spits on his father, then falls on his sword, marrying Antigone in death. In a tragedy, *climax* means the main characters go down to defeat.

The Falling Action

Following the climax, the rest of the drama is devoted to showing what the characters' lives are like after this major change in their fortunes.

After Percinet has routed the "kidnappers," the fathers tearfully agree to forget their quarrel, to take down the wall, and to permit the marriage. Since the young lovers are impressed by the change in their fathers, the tension between the generations is thoroughly resolved.

But the resolution for Creon is of course thoroughly catastrophic. Returning to the palace with the body of Haemon, he finds that his wife, having heard of the tragedy in the prison, has killed herself. Creon asks that he be exiled.

Tragedy and Tragicomedy Compared

At this point we can profit by comparing the resolutions achieved in our four plays. Shakespeare's play, as much a tragedy as Sophocles', also ends in catastrophe. Goaded on by the villainous machinations of Iago, Othello murders Desdemona. Only then does he discover that he has been deceived. He kills himself and Iago is led away to be tortured to death.

Chayefsky's play, like Rostand's, also ends on a positive note. However, we would be tempted to call it not a comedy but a tragicomedy. The old lady does get a job, in the garment industry, but she makes a serious error in sewing sleeves and is fired. Seemingly defeated, she consents to move in with George and Annie. But she cannot sleep. As morning breaks, she leaves again to look for work because "work is the meaning" of life. She has not "lost" but neither has she "won." In any event, the emphasis has been not on the result but on the struggle. Such ambiguity characterizes modern tragicomedy: an interest neither in happy ending nor in tragic ending but only in the ongoing struggle and the dignity it imparts.

Nontraditional Dramatic Structure

Have you felt, without knowing why exactly, that there's something artificial about traditional plot? Can we be sure that such a pattern corresponds to real life just because it makes for exciting theater? Since it's the same pattern used over and over, why is it imposed on situations actually quite various?

Look at the basic assumptions in the traditional plot. It assumes we can establish causal relations between events, single out some events as absolutely more significant than others, and extract from them the meaning of life and judgments about good and evil. It assumes that catharsis in the theater is socially desirable. And because catharsis must be achieved, all events must converge on a crescendo climax. By emphasizing sharp external conflict, the plot assigns major importance to confrontation, to adversary relations. It encourages us to view life not as a spectrum ranging from controversy to collaboration, but as black-and-white opposition.

Many dramatists and novelists in modern times deeply distrust the motive behind traditional plotting. Emile Zola felt it is designed to make certain comfortable but false beliefs appear as universal truths—for example, that evil is always punished and virtue always rewarded, that order and logic prevail in life and in history. In other words, traditional plot is prefabricated to reassure us, subliminally, that all's right with the world, a form of cultural brainwashing.

"I mistrust . . . people . . . when their stories hold together," says a typical anti-hero in Ernest Hemingway's novel *The Sun Also Rises*. The anti-hero suspects that story has been imposed on facts to make sense out of them, that story inevitably reshapes the facts.

Hence the anti-hero doubts that history happened that way, for he sees "history" as the plot, the design, into which the historian has arranged the facts. For centuries, for example, all past history was reconstructed to conform to the Christian view of man's place and future in God's scheme: the Divine Creation as background exposition, the temptation in the Garden of Eden as the initial moment, the Crucifixion as the climax, post-Crucifixion life as falling action, man's attainment of Heaven or Hell (comedy or tragedy!) as the denouement. Christian Europe actually dated all history as occurring before or after Christ, so that Sophocles, for example, is seen as living backwards (from 495 to 406 B.C.), his entire life pointing toward an event that had nothing to do with his culture.

As Tom F. Driver, theology professor, observes in his book *Romantic Quest and Modern Query*, this *master-plot* of history has lost its authority for modern man. And he says that dramatists like Samuel Beckett have made us aware that not just this particular plot is "waning in power, but also the very notion of *any* plot as a model for the interpretation of human existence."

But even before Beckett, novelists like Zola and dramatists like Anton Chekhov had tried out other models, shaping each novel or play not according to traditional patterns but according to the implications of the subject matter.

You can get some idea of how to analyze nontraditional dramatic structure if we examine two typical "plotless" plays.

Story of a "Slice of Life" Drama

Lubov Ranevskaya returns to Russia to find that her estate, including her famous cherry orchard, must be auctioned off to pay her debts. Her brother Gaev hopes they will inherit some money, or a wealthy relative will come to their aid, or Lubov's daughter Anya will marry a rich man. Pischik, a neighbor who was rescued from similar straits when the railroad bought some of his land, hopes some such development will save Lubov. And Varya, her adopted daughter, believes God will save them. Only Lopakin, a peasant's son who is now a rich merchant, has a practical solution. Lubov could cut down the orchard, build summer cottages, rent them out, and live on the income. This Lubov cannot bear to see, but she has no other plan to save her property.

During a day in the meadow, and during a ball that Madame Ranevskaya gives on the very night of the auction, we learn of the views, attitudes, and problems of several members of her entourage. A German governess broods over her origins and history. Trofimov, perennial university student and vague idealist, claims to be "above love" but shyly courts the light-hearted Anya. The silly maid Dunyasha has been proposed to by the poor clerk Yepihodov, but she hopes to marry Yasha, the valet bored with provincial life.

Lopakin arrives at the ball, shamefaced, to announce he has bought the estate and will clear the orchard. Gaev will have to work in a bank, and Varya as a housekeeper. Lubov will return to Paris, her finances slightly bolstered by Pischik's latest stroke of luck: Geologists have found white clay on his land and he can settle his debts to Lubov. Yasha is delighted to accompany Madame abroad, while Dunyasha is resigned to life with a dull clerk. The family scatters, forgetting to provide for old Firs, the footman, who falls on a sofa as the first sounds of the axe are heard from the orchard.

That's the subject matter of Anton Chekhov's *The Cherry Orchard* (1904), a classic of world drama.

Structure of a "Slice of Life" Drama

Although the sale of the orchard is the turning point in the lives of the characters, it is by no means a crisis in the traditional sense of the word. No one has struggled for or against the sale; there is no major conflict, no rising action, no complication, no mounting tension before the sale. It was a foregone conclusion before the curtain rose. In a certain sense, the play is devoted mainly to the demoralizing *effects* of the sale situation. No one has had the will to take a stand as a protagonist in any cause. And neither is Lopakin an antagonist: He had no plans to buy the orchard until, at the auction, he realized that a business rival was about to win the bidding.

Instead of a series of linked events leading up to and resolved by a climax, we have rather a series of loosely related, diffuse conversations in low-key situations. Chekhov presents us with a "slice of life," a cross-section of a certain society at a certain point in its history. Instead of action we have circumstance; instead of suspense we have resignation. The resulting "inaction" is utterly faithful to an actual historical situation and provides us with one of the great "mood pieces" of modern theater.

Story of an "Absurdist" Drama

Near a solitary, leafless tree, two tramps meet, as always, to wait for Godot. Gogo struggles with his boots and Didi fusses with his hat. Gogo takes naps and tries afterward to talk of his dreams, but Didi won't listen. Didi ponders the different ways the four Gospels treat the two thieves crucified with Jesus. The tramps consider separation or suicide but postpone action. Pozzo, owner of the surrounding land, pulled by his serf Lucky whom he has on a leash, pauses to eat his lunch in the company of the tramps. He talks of the value of clock time, and of selling Lucky, who was once his teacher. Lucky cries, but when Gogo offers him a handkerchief, he kicks him. Pozzo commands Lucky, "Think, pig!"

and the serf launches into a long outburst, in mock legalistic, scholarly jib-berish, about man's past, present, and future, and God's favoritism and partial-ity. After the master and slave leave, a goat-boy tells the tramps: Godot will come tomorrow.

When the second act opens, the tree has several leaves. Waiting for Godot, the tramps pass the time with games, philosophical talk, and calisthenics. Pozzo, now blind, and Lucky, now speechless, enter and collapse. After Didi orates on the rare chance he and Gogo have to *do* something, they themselves fall before they can raise Pozzo and Lucky. Pozzo, now impatient with all questions about clock time, goads Lucky into resuming their incessant travel. Didi so-liloquizes on his predicament and seems on the verge of a major insight when the boy interrupts with the same message. The tramps plan to hang themselves tomorrow if Godot does not come.

That's a summary of what goes on in Beckett's *Waiting for Godot* (1953), perhaps the most influential drama of the late twentieth century.

Structure of an "Absurdist" Drama

Once again we have a play with no conflict in the traditional sense, no development, complication, or resolution of whatever problems are posed. Whatever action there is — or inaction — seems to be more symbolic, more abstract than realistic. Nevertheless, the play's structure seems to carry great significance. What does it mean that Acts I and II are quite similar in form and content? In both acts, the tramps wait for Godot, Pozzo and Lucky pass through, a boy brings a message, the tramps decide to come back and wait again tomorrow. Still, within this repetition of overall pattern, the second act does comprise some differences. Didi does seem closer to understanding. Pozzo and Lucky have changed radically. But we don't know the exact *causes* of their change, nor do we know why Godot does not come, or, indeed, who Godot is. Both the incessantly active characters and the bored, passive characters seem equal in defeat in a seemingly absurd, meaningless world. And again, there is less communicated to us by action, more by mood and condition.

Evaluating Nontraditional Structure

Notice that our process of evaluation here has been twofold. We have made certain the play is not plotted according to traditional patterns. And we have simply described its original pattern and its effect. Later of course we shall discuss further the way structure affects theme.

Characterization

Plot and characterization, as we have seen with fiction, are two sides of the same coin. Plot is a sequence of events that challenge the characters to grow; but the characters, of course, can also initiate events. Plot and characterization, then, can be discussed only in terms of each other.

But this does not mean necessarily that every play will place equal emphasis on plot and character. In this respect, let us compare Chayefsky's *The Mother* with Rostand's *The Romancers.*

In *The Mother*, an aged widow discovers that, despite setbacks, she cannot violate her own nature. She must work to provide the circumstances she needs to regain her dignity. A determined daughter, who believes herself to be self-sacrificing, is revealed actually to have vindictive reasons for wanting to help her mother. The daughter grows at least to the extent that she can, at last, express her admiration for her mother's need for independence. The son-in-law develops as a man who can learn more and more about his wife's weaknesses and still love her. In every case, Chayefsky has deepened his characterization by plunging his people into *inner* as well as *outer* conflict.

Does Rostand's play measure up in this respect? The two fathers and the lovers have struggled with outer circumstances, all have changed their life situations, but none of them has struggled with any inner weaknesses. None of them, in short, has undergone any profound change of personality.

The Romancers, then, is literally a situation play: We have enjoyed the outcome of the *plot. The Mother* is a character drama: We have appreciated the difficulties and the rewards in growth of character. *The Romancers* stresses plot for *action's sake; The Mother* fully explores action for *characterization's sake.*

Essentials of Characterization

Your *first question*, then, when you evaluate a playwright's characterization, is this: Are the central characters called upon by events to solve inner as well as outer problems? A *second important concern* is: Are all major actions properly motivated?

You could tell by our plot summary that Shakespeare quickly provides a reason for Iago's desire to hurt Othello and Cassio. Othello has appointed Cassio to the rank that Iago believes he himself deserves.

Consider also the scene in *The Mother* where the old lady is fired by her boss in the garment factory. Chayefsky takes great pains to make us understand the human reasons behind the boss's action, even though he is only a minor character. Earlier in the play we have heard the boss begging his brother-in-law for bigger, better-paying contracts. The brother-in-law agrees but only if the boss can make the deadline on today's job. The boss tries to lash his work force into greater speed. The old lady does sew her quota of sleeves but (dramatic reversal!) she made them all "left-hand," none "right-hand"! The brother-in-law uses the ensuing delay as his excuse for canceling the bigger contracts. Now the boss needs a scapegoat. Chayefsky's stage direction reads: *years of accumulated humiliation and resentment flood . . . out of him.* The scene closes with the boss yelling "Fire her! Fire her!"

Characters are more credible, then, if their actions are well motivated and reflect internal as well as external problems. A *third question* is: Has the playwright made each character distinctly different? Notice how swiftly Beckett begins to differentiate his tramps. Didi fusses with his hat, Gogo with his boots. More gradually, of course, the author can distinguish characters by the quality of their speech: Didi in his pensiveness, Pozzo by his pomposity.

Functions of Characters

You will find it helpful too to keep a *fourth question* in mind: What function does each character perform in the development of other characters and in the advancement of the action and theme?

The question is easier to answer with main characters. In opposing each other, Antigone and Creon represent the claims of the conscience in conflict with the claims of the law. And they both illustrate for us the tragedy of rigidity of attitude. Each is so self-righteous that he or she makes it impossible for anyone to achieve a working compromise between their views.

The function of noncentral characters may require more thought on your part. Consider the role of the palace guard in *Antigone*. On the level of plot, he has advanced the action: He brings to Creon the news that someone has performed burial rites on the body of Polynices. But think too of his function on the level of characterization. In provoking the anger of Creon, the guard has made it clear to us that Creon cannot tolerate any difference of opinion, that indeed he cannot even keep his head. The way he treats a mere messenger makes us wonder about Antigone's chances of being judged fairly or even of being understood.

The guard's psychological function, then, is an important one in drama: Minor character though he is, he functions to provoke a revealing action out of a major character.

See too how many functions Ismene performs. On the level of action, she serves in the opening scene as *confidante*: that is, a minor character in whom a main character (in this case, Antigone) can confide, thus revealing to the audience what her (his) intentions are. On the level of characterization, Ismene serves as a *foil*. She illuminates Antigone's character by contrast. Passive, obedient to authority, a lover of the quiet life, she emphasizes the fact that Antigone is active, independent, willing to take a stand in major public issues. Later in the play, Ismene dramatizes for us the internal conflict a person can suffer when torn between duty to family and duty to the state.

You will be safe if you assume that almost any character can serve as a foil for a main character. You would soon realize that Haemon is a perfect foil for his father. Just in being reasonable, tactful, and open-minded, Haemon makes clearer to us that Creon is the opposite. For example, Creon is furious at the very idea of an assertive, independent woman; Haemon is in love with one.

Of course, you should especially expect that the antagonist and protagonist will be foils for each other. We quickly appreciate the craftiness, complexity, and subtlety of Iago, and the openness, simplicity, and naivete of Othello, because they are developed in opposition.

Even the *walk-on*, the minor character who appears briefly or only in the background, will contribute to the overall effect, advance the action, or serve as a contrast. Thus in John Millington Synge's *Riders to the Sea*, several villagers enter the cottage of the bereaved Maurya. They kneel and join in the keening, a ritual wailing for the dead. Their functions are to provide local color, to show the Irish attitude toward death and bereavement, and to effect a contrast between the neighbors' formal, dutiful mourning and the family's passionate, helpless mourning.

Methods of Characterization

The dramatist can reveal and develop his characters in three ways. He may (1) have them described by a narrator, (2) have them describe and discuss each other, or (3) have them describe and reveal themselves in action.

Description by a Narrator

For special effects, and under certain circumstances, the playwright may make use of a narrator. Thus, in Thornton Wilder's *Our Town* (1938), the stage manager lingers on stage after the play opens; he explains the action and comments on the people involved in the love story of George Gibbs and Emily Webb. And in Tennessee Williams' *The Glass Menagerie* (1945), we see the whole story of Tom's nagging mother and his crippled sister as he recalls their life together. Other characters describe him, of course, and we are free to judge all characters for ourselves, but it's Tom's point of view that dominates.

The playwright finds the radio play the most natural medium for the use of the narrator. Since the radio play can be staged only in our mind from cues supplied through our ears, it requires an on-the-spot announcer or observer who tells us what *he* sees, identifies for us the other voices that we hear, and of course *describes* those speakers for us. In Archibald MacLeish's classic radio verse-drama, *The Fall of the City* (1937), the narrator is a journalist covering the public's reaction to the imminent arrival of a conqueror. It is the narrator who describes for us the horse-raisers ogling the girls in the crowd, the arrival of an exhausted messenger, the appearance of the priests. It is from the journalist that we get verbal clues to build our mental image of a general wearing a feathered coat and of the conqueror himself, "broad as a brass door."

Description by Others

But in the typical stage play, the dramatist does not use a narrator. Thus when he has the various characters describe and discuss each other, they can exert more of a direct influence on the audience. Consider the dramatic effects of Iago's describing Cassio to Roderigo *before* we have seen Cassio:

> Forsooth, a great arithmetician,
> One Michael Cassio, a Florentine
> (A fellow almost damned in a fair wife),
> That never set a squadron in the field,
> Nor the division of a battle knows
> More than a spinster . . .
> . . . Mere prattle, without practice,
> Is all his soldiership. But he, sir, had
> the election . . .

Precisely because this seems to be a blend of fact and opinion about Cassio, it piques our curiosity to find out which is which; and it shows us where he stands with Iago, thus advancing characterization as well as suspense.

By the end of Act I, Iago's description of the main character, Othello, takes on extraordinary significance. . .

> The Moor is of a free and open nature
> That thinks men honest that but seem
>   to be so,
> And will as tenderly be led by the nose
> As asses are.

. . . for Iago's description not only sums up our own first impressions of Othello's "free and open nature," it also gives us a strong hint of his tragic flaw, and of his fate.

Perhaps one character's description of another can provide the most poignant example of dramatic irony. Near the end of the play, when Desdemona lies dead, Othello describes to Emilia the man who informed him of his wife's infidelity. It was:

> My friend, thy husband; honest,
>   honest Iago.

We watch Othello intently now to see how he will react when he discovers what we have long known.

Self-Description

By having his characters describe themselves, the playwright can fill in much of his background exposition very quickly and, of course, again exploit the device for suspense and irony. But a character must be well motivated to be so autobiographical. At the very opening of *The Cherry Orchard*, Lopakin and Dunyasha impatiently await the arrival of Lubov who has been gone for five years. Wondering what "she's like now," Lopakin naturally thinks back to the time he first met her. A boy of 15, he had come into Lubov's yard with a bloody nose.

> She was still young and slender. She led me to the washbasin . . . right in this very room . . . right here in the nursery.

We look around the room too. The memory of the past is linked to the present.

> She said, "Don't cry, little peasant, it will heal before your wedding day."

Lopakin suddenly pauses. This is the first suspenseful moment of the play. Yes, he realizes aloud, he *was* a peasant, and he looks (as we look) at the fine coat and shoes he is wearing. That's just the first shock. Now he describes himself as "a pig in a pastry shop," for though he's rich now, he's still a peasant. He flips the pages of a book he's been reading. He comments:

> I didn't understand any of it.

In having Lopakin describe himself, Chekhov has given us background information not just about one person but about a society in rapid transition; and he has triggered long-range suspense. What are the immediate implications of these class distinctions Lopakin is so self-conscious about? Has he ever married? Was that an unacknowledged reason for the pause?

Beckett also stiffens quick exposition with suspense when he has Didi describe himself and Gogo in *Waiting for Godot.*

> . . . what's the good of losing heart now . . . We should have thought of it in the nineties . . . Hand in hand from the top of the Eiffel Tower, among the first. We were respectable in those days. Now it's too late. They wouldn't even let us up.

Exposition: We know that the tramps are so old they could have ascended the Parisian landmark when it was new, and that in those days they were not tramps. *Theme:* This is a world in which people habitually use the Tower for suicide jumps. *Suspense:* Will the tramps commit suicide some other way?

Sophocles can use a single line of self-description to accomplish several dramatic purposes, as when he has Antigone tell Ismene:

> . . . For me, the doer, death is best.

She has summed up her own self-image in two words (the doer), contrasted herself with her sister, and triggered suspense: Can she live up to her self-image? to the threat of death?

Self-Revelation

Our examples of characters describing themselves have so far all been expository in nature, and all rather deliberately spoken early in the play. Far more dramatic is what characters say and do under stress, in the midst of well-developed, ongoing action. When the palace guard returns with his prisoner, Antigone, Creon says:

> Now what must I measure up to?

He intends apparently to comment on the heavy duties laid on a ruler, but notice too the unwitting self-revelation: He is not very secure in his job.

Especially revealing of course is what a character says and does at the catastrophe. This is the point in the action at which he gains final insight into the truth not only of his situation but of his own character. After Othello has been apprized of the truth about Iago, he revises his self-image and tells the others now to

>   . . . speak
> Of one that loved not wisely, but too well;
> Of one not easily jealous, but, being
>   wrought,
> Perplexed in the extreme . . .

And now he chooses to punish himself in a highly symbolic manner. Leaning over the body of Desdemona,

> *He stabs himself.*
>
>   * * *
> I kissed thee ere I killed thee.
>   No way but this—
> Killing myself, to die upon a kiss.

He falls across his wife and dies.

As a tragic hero defeated by an alliance of outer and inner enemies, Othello measures up to the climax. But as an anti-hero, Didi backs down. After Pozzo and Lucky's very disturbing visit, Didi stares at the sleeping Gogo and wonders: If someone were to stare at Didi now as Didi stares at Gogo, would that someone conclude that Didi *also*

> . . . is sleeping, he knows nothing, let him sleep on. (*Pause*) I can't go on! (*Pause*) What have I said?

This is the closest Didi comes to accusing himself of self-deception. Not only does he correct himself, as though he cannot allow himself to *say* that, but now he is completely distracted by the arrival of the boy and lapses back into habit: He *can* go on in self-deception, and he does.

Evaluating Characterization

Getting ready to discuss how your playwright portrays his characters, you should consider:

☆ Does he stress plot for action's sake or exploit plot for characterization's sake? In other words, is his play a *situation drama* or a *character drama*?

☆ Does he use a good enough balance of *inner and outer conflict* in his characterization to approximate the psychological difficulties of real life?

☆ Are all his main characters *credibly motivated*?

☆ Is each character *distinctly different,* for example, in speech, manner, psychology? *Do the main characters develop*?

☆ What *function* does each character perform in advancing the action, developing other characters, and formulating the theme?

☆ Is there enough *contrast in character portrayals* so that we can see alternatives of conduct that were open to the main characters?

☆ Which *methods of characterization* does your dramatist use effectively: Having characters describe and discuss each other? Having them describe and reveal themselves? If your playwright uses a narrator, what are the special effects or reasons?

☆ How much do we learn from the fate of the characters about *human nature* and the *human condition*?

Applying what you have learned so far, you might take notes about Othello, Desdemona, Didi, and Gogo, for example, like this:

Othello

Through his own action and speech, and through the comments of others, Othello is revealed as a person of social importance who rides high on his strengths until he runs into a situation in which he is tripped up by his worst fault. Ironically—and irony is the heart of drama—his tragic flaw is almost a direct consequence of, or a complement to, his heroic strengths.

Othello's fame rests on his courage to act swiftly and decisively in military situations. The alternatives are clear. Sides are neatly drawn. The enemy is out in the open and fights according to the rules of warfare. Othello sees himself as someone at his best in tests of violence. To succeed as a general, he assumes that where there's smoke, there's fire. Just to be in doubt, he boasts, is to be resolved. In combat, suspending judgment until all evidence is in could be fatal. Othello is a famous warrior because he strikes fast.

Now, however, the soldier who has lived mainly with men makes a conquest in a new, unknown field—serious relations with a woman. He talks of Desdemona as he thinks of all reality: in grand but simple terms. She is worth a world of solid topaz, her skin is smooth as "monumental alabaster," her wit is "so high." Life is so sublimely simple for him that he naively feels he has solved all his problems and reached a plateau of joy.

Othello's tragic flaw—his ignorance of human psychology, including self-ignorance—makes him blindly vulnerable to Iago the Tempter. Iago can poison Othello's mind with suggestions about his "ignorance" of the sexual code of Venetian women, about how if Desdemona is so unconventional as to marry a Moor, she can easily do other "unnatural" things. Othello is overwhelmed by how unworldly he is compared to Iago who

> . . . knows all qualities . . .
> Of human dealings.

Othello's sense of inferiority in those "dealings" leads to his insecurity. He becomes pathetically aware of how he is much older than his wife, lacks her culture, and is a foreigner. Insecurity leads to jealousy. The growing complexity of "human dealings" shatters the noble simplicity that was the secret of his success. He reacts to the threat of chaos with military violence, thus regaining, at least in his own eyes, his nobility. Even in his last speech, he is still so self-ignorant as to describe himself as "one not easily jealous."

Othello is, in other words, a typical "tragic hero": a person of social prominence whose downfall is caused by an alliance of an outer enemy and inner weakness.

Desdemona

She is even more of a tragic victim than Othello, for whom, in some respects, she serves as a foil. She is more rational under stress than he is, and suffers greater torments with greater poise. It was she who took the initiative in an area where he hesitated—courtship. It was she who saw that marriage to the Moor would involve a break with her father and she accepted it. She gives Othello the benefit of the doubt at a time she has the right to yield to her feelings and be as irrational as he.

But in some respects she is almost as naive as he is, so that her tragic flaw reinforces his. She innocently sees him as too noble to be jealous and she actually thinks wives are incapable of infidelity. Long after Othello has changed, she continues to relate to him as though he is still his old self. She too cracks under the pressures of Iago's plot and in terror twice fibs to her husband about a handkerchief she has lost. She cannot know that Iago has made evil use of it. She is the victim of a man's world. Her father cannot distinguish between independence and disloyalty; to punish her, he helps poison her husband's mind against her. And her husband takes other men's word as more believable than his wife's.

Didi and Gogo

These two tramps are so obviously *foils* for each other that it makes sense to discuss them together. As a matter of fact, the more we discuss them, the more we are tempted to consider them as two halves of the same character. Beckett reveals their separate (and related) natures through the use of symbolic spectacle, tag-names, description by other characters, and self-revelation.

Gogo fusses with his footwear and Didi with his headgear. Thus Beckett draws our attention to the fact that Gogo is earthier, more in touch with the physical world, while Didi is more intellectual, more at home in the world of abstract ideas.

This distinction is intensified when we see that Gogo loves to take naps and wants to recount his dreams, but Didi refuses to hear them. Gogo emerges as the proponent of the unconscious, instinctive, irrational, sensuous forces in man, while Didi stands for man's conscious and logical powers.

Beckett reinforces some of these distinctions through tag-names. Gogo is a nickname for Estragon, French for tarragon, a wormwood grown for its foliage which is used for making pickles and vinegar. The pungent but earthy flavor perfectly suits the boot-wearing Gogo. His nickname suits his restlessness: He is always the one of the tramps who wants to *go, go,* leave, *not* wait for Godot. Didi, on the other hand, the nickname for Vladimir, sounds like *dis-dis,* from the French verb *dire,* to speak. It is "speak-speak," the logical one, who always restrains "Gogo," the intuitive one.

If they are two parts of the same personality, then, Didi seems to stand for the Ego, the social, logical self, while Gogo represents the Id, or the subjective, irrational, unconscious self. But D*id*i contains *id,* and Gog*o,* *ego.* Is this Beckett's way of indicating that they are inextricably related to each other?

But alas they are related too much in conflict, too little in collaboration. They perfectly symbolize, then, the tragedy of modern man, self-divided between his mind-soul and his body-senses, torn by inner conflict that paralyzes him.

Their crippling conflict between intellect and instinct is just one of their problems. Another is that they are waiting for salvation from outside themselves — perhaps precisely because they are immobilized by conflicts inside themselves. They are waiting to be saved by Godot, who keeps postponing his coming until tomorrow. Gogo just instinctively wants to discontinue this passive vigil but Didi, as mind, as the proponent of social logic, is in command. Just once, as we have seen, does Didi venture toward the insight that *waiting* for Godot is the equivalent of *sleeping.* Just once, in other words, has it occurred to him to find salvation inside himself. Having missed this opportunity to become awake, he continues to sleep.

Significance of Characterization

Through his characters, Shakespeare signifies (1) generally, that in time of stress, a tragic flaw can undo a person's strengths, and (2) specifically, a person strong and glorious in the martial arts may be dangerously inept in "human dealings" at close range.

Through his characters, Beckett signifies (1) generally, that modern man's mind is dangerously divorced from his instincts, and (2) specifically, that he may remain neurotically passive, hopelessly waiting for help from the outside, unless he reunites his own psyche.

Characterization and Theme

In other words, just as we found it in our study of fiction, so in drama: Character development may provide our major clues to the author's theme.

Language in Drama

You have probably noted — maybe in our remarks about Didi's hat and Gogo's boots—how spectacle can signify in drama. And you know, from watching teleplays and screenplays, how sound effects can dramatize. But you will readily agree that language contributes the major share to the overall quality of a play; language serves as the main cumulative and unifying force.

Language and Action

The title character in Chayefsky's *The Mother* stares through a rain-splashed window. Her alarm goes off at 6:30 A.M. Entirely through visual effects, we observe that she is disturbed by the weather. But we do not know exactly how the rain has upset her plans until Annie arrives and they *discuss* them in detail. Again, we see the old lady spending the following night in a chair, fully dressed, sleepless. But we do not know what decisions are percolating in her gray head until she *announces* them to Annie.

Language as Characterization

Language, then, can play a vital role in advancing the action. Language is also a major means of revealing the unique makeup of a character — how he/she differs from other persons, how he/she develops as a person.

In his dialogue, even in talk between main characters, Shakespeare gives them speeches that distinguish their moods and personalities. In the following exchange, the Duke tries to get Desdemona's father to accept the elopement.

Shakespeare casts the Duke's advice into very dogged, formal, administrative pronouncements.

> *Duke.*   Let me speak like yourself and lay a sentence
> Which, as a grise or step, may help these lovers
> Into your favor.
> When remedies are past, the griefs are ended
> By seeing the worst, which late on hopes depended.
> To mourn a mischief that is past and gone
> Is the next way to draw new mischief on.
> What cannot be preserved when fortune takes,
> Patience her injury a mock'ry makes.
> The robbed that smiles steals something from the thief;
> He robs himself that spends a bootless grief.

But for her father Brabantio's reply, Shakespeare uses more nimble language, bitter and sarcastic:

> *Brabantio.*   So let the Turk of Cyprus us beguile:
> We lose it not, so long as we can smile.
> He bears the sentence well that nothing bears
> But the free comfort which from thence he hears;
> But he bears both the sentence and the sorrow
> That to pay grief must of poor patience borrow.
> These sentences, to sugar, or to gall,
> Being strong on both sides, are equivocal.
> But words are words: I never yet did hear
> That the bruised heart was pierced through the ear.
> I humbly beseech you, proceed to the affairs of state.

Not bound to the ten-syllable line, as was Shakespeare, the modern verse-dramatist can vary the length of his line to help distinguish between people and between their states of mind. Thus, in his *Fall of the City*, MacLeish uses choppy, breathless lines for the speech of the conscientious but exhausted messenger:

> Be well warned!
> He comes to you slightly
> Slanting and sprinting
> Hinting and shadowing:
> Sly in his chiding:
> A hard lot:
> A late rider:
> Watch! I have said to you.

But he uses longer lines, a more varied, involved syntax, for the speech of the orator:

> Those who win by the spear are the spear-toters.
> And what do they win? Spears! What else is there?
> If their hands let go they have nothing to hold by.
> They are no more free than a paralytic propped against a tree is.

From his earliest work, like *Waiting for Godot*, Beckett has also fashioned a characteristic mode of speech for each character. Gogo, for example, speaks mainly in simple, declarative sentences, Didi in more complex sentence patterns. This suits Gogo's tendency to free associate, to speak more passionately, and Didi's tendency to use language mainly to pose and solve problems. Gogo's language accepts chaos and mystery; Didi's language struggles for clarity.

Figures of Speech

Irony

Language, of course, can contribute largely to *dramatic irony*, that theatrical tension produced by the dramatist's exploiting the difference between illusion and reality. The playwright, for example, may have arranged his scenes so that the audience knows certain things that certain characters do not know. The tension consists in our watching how those characters function with only incomplete knowledge of the situation.

Verbal irony is irony that consists specifically in the language (rather than generally in the situation). A character may say one thing and mean another; or may say something that is ironic to us because we know he is speaking from ignorance; or may say something that appears to be true but later proves to be false; or he may say more than he realizes, as we noted when Creon says:

> Now what must I measure up to?

Two samples from Iago's speeches to Othello will suffice to show the nature and power of verbal irony. Iago is slowly arousing Othello's suspicions about Cassio; he is pretending to be hesitant about blackening Cassio's reputation.

> Good name in man and woman, dear my lord,
> Is the immediate jewel of their souls.
> Who steals my purse steals trash; 'tis something, nothing;
> 'Twas mine, 'tis his, and has been slave to thousands;
> But he that filches from me my good name
> Robs me of that which not enriches him
> And makes me poor indeed.

Now we know what Othello does not know: that Iago does not deserve his "good name" and that Cassio does his. Most ironic of all is the fact that Iago is using beautiful truths to establish ugly lies as truth. Worse, naive Othello cannot see that the beautiful language is veiling a villainous plot in the making. As Othello begins to writhe in jealousy Iago says:

> O, beware, my lord, of jealousy!
> It is the green-eyed monster

Again, we know that Iago wants Othello not to "beware" of jealousy but rather to yield to it. You can take it as axiomatic: Irony is one of the main elements of drama. A play lacking in dramatic and verbal irony is a play lacking in depth, resonance, and tension.

Metaphor

Irony is the first of three main types of figures of speech essential to drama. The second is *metaphor*, a comparison, a form of expression that likens unlike things. Thus Iago expresses the value of one's "good name" by likening it to the "jewel" of one's soul. He makes jealousy ugly and foolish by identifying it with a "green-eyed monster." When the comparison is established with actual use of an equal sign (like, as) we call the metaphor a *simile*. Thus, after Othello has killed Desdemona, he and Desdemona's maid Emilia engage in a sharp exchange of similes:

> *Othello.*   She was false as water.
> *Emilia.*   Thou
>   art rash as fire . . .
> As ignorant as dirt!

A successful metaphor speeds up the audience's comprehension; it makes a quick association between the known and the unknown, between past experience and the present moment. Since we all know that water is unstable, fire unpredictable, and dirt mindless, we can feel with instant excitement just what the characters mean. The excitement comes from the shock of being forced to see a relationship between two unrelated things. The excitement makes us feel closer, emotionally, to the character who uses the metaphor.

Symbol

The most suggestive, compact, and powerful of all figures of speech is the symbol: that is, a thing, place, person, or situation that stands for something else, something larger than itself. Often it is a material thing that represents something immaterial.

Early in Chekhov's play *The Bear*, when Popova is reminded of how her late husband used to ride his horse, Toby, we hear this speech:

> *Popova.*   . . . Tell them to give Toby an extra bag of oats today.

Later, when businessman Smirnov tells Popova that he supplied her husband with oats we hear:

> *Popova.*   . . . Luba, don't forget to tell them to give Toby an extra bag of oats.

And at play's end, when Luba finds Popova in Smirnov's arms, we hear:

> *Popova.*   . . . Luba, tell them in the stable not to give Toby any oats today.

In other words, at crucial points in the action, Chekhov has used Popova's attitudes toward a bag of oats to symbolize her changing attitudes toward her late husband. Dramatists can use symbols to represent the overall quality of an experience, or a character's state of mind, or even the theme of the play. Unless they employed symbols, playwrights could not hope to pack so much reinforced meaning into such a short work as a drama.

Dramatic Pacing through Language

Drama, like fiction, must ebb and flow, speed up and slow down, rise and fall in tension. Language can affect this dramatic pacing not only through the content but through its rhythms and shapes. For example, as the dramatist develops a scene he can vary the length of the speeches. In *Antigone*, as the tension increases, Sophocles uses shorter speeches until finally characters are engaged in *stichomythy* (dialogue in which each speech is a single line of the same length). Stichomythy speeds up the action, gives it a staccato, duel-like, blow-for-blow quality.

> Creon.   What cliché emerges from your lips?
> Tiresias.   Better than wealth is good sound advice.
> Creon.   Worse than poverty is folly.
> Tiresias.   And that's the illness you're infected with.
> Creon.   I hate to be impolite to a prophet.
> Tiresias.   Too late. You've already called me a liar.
> Creon.   Because all prophets are after money.
> Tiresias.   And all tyrants are after power.

As the conflict subsides, or as one character takes over, or the scene moves toward its resolution, the speeches expand again in length.

Beckett develops stichomythy for varied effects. In *Endgame*, he uses it like Sophocles—to tighten the tension. But in *Waiting for Godot*, he uses it to effect harmony. When Didi and Gogo cease their quibbling and bickering, their different language styles blend into one: They match each other's words, phrases, or sentences in stichomythic parallelism.

> Vladimir.   We could do our exercises.
> Estragon.   Our movements.
> Vladimir.   Our elevations.
> Estragon.   Our relaxations.
> Vladimir.   Our elongations.
> Estragon.   Our relaxations.
> Vladimir.   To warm us up.
> Estragon.   To calm us down.

Before and after such duets, Didi and Gogo are likely to speak in nonparallel statements, Gogo in simple sentences and Didi in complex sentences.

Language as Mood Music

Language has sound as well as sense, and in the hands of a good dramatic artist, the sound reinforces the sense, the sound contributes to the mood. In every line that they write, Shakespeare and Beckett make it clear that they are choosing appropriate sounds, carefully arranging their vowels and consonants. The magic of Othello's line

> Keep up your bright swords, for the
> dew will rust them

comes partly from the great variety of tones—eight vowel sounds—concentrated into a mere eleven words! And notice that a seemingly simple line like Iago's

> I know my price, I am worth no
> worse a place

is actually an intensely interwoven succession of sounds: *price* and *place* half rhyme through their consonant sounds (*p--ce*), *worth* and *worse* through their vowel sound (*or*). And the "I" sound and "no" (*know, no*) sound are both repeated.

Shakespeare uses such craftsmanship sparingly in calm statements but lavishly in passionate speeches. Notice how full "o" and "u" sounds, piercing "i" sounds, and thick consonants help build up the mood of Othello's famous farewell to fame and career.

> Farewell the plumed troop, and the
>   big wars
> That make ambition virtue!
>   O farewell!
> Farewell the neighing steed and
>   the shrill trump,
> The spirit-stirring drum, the ear-
>   piercing fife,
> The royal banner, and all quality,
> Pride, pomp and circumstance of
>   glorious war!
> And O ye mortal engines whose rude
>   throats
> Th' immortal Jove's dread clamors
>   counterfeit,
> Farewell! Othello's occupation's
>   gone!

Shakespeare even makes artistic use of the differences in the duration of words. In the following passage, Othello speaks 42 short words, all but one of them one syllable long! Then suddenly he breaks into multisyllabic words.

> It is the cause, it is the cause, my soul.
> Let me not name it to you, you chaste
>   stars!
> It is the cause. Yet I'll not shed her
>   blood,
> Nor scar that whiter skin of hers
>   than snow,
> And smooth as monumental
>   alabaster.

The musical effect of the sudden shift from monosyllables to polysyllables is one of poignant contrast.

Evaluating Dramatic Language

You are now armed with key questions for judging a playwright's success in putting language to dramatic use.

☆ Has the dramatist created a *characteristic manner of speaking* for each person?

☆ How much does the dialogue contribute to the *pacing of the action*?

☆ How successfully does the playwright use figures of speech: *verbal irony, metaphor, symbol*? Are each character's figures of speech true to his or her personality? Do they create a corresponding emotional excitement in the audience?

☆ Do the *sound* and *rhythm* of the language help create the *moods* of the play?

☆ How do the *sound* and *sense* combined contribute to the *theme*?

Spectacle and Sound Effects

You *see* in the theater before you *hear.* Spectacle almost always precedes dialogue. After the opening moments, though, spectacle may assume minor importance, as in the traditional stageplay, or major importance, as in contemporary "total theater." There has never been any question about the prominence of spectacle in the screenplay and teleplay, whose technology makes them audio-visual by nature.

Looking back over some of the works we've been studying here, we can consider them now in an order that chronicles the growing significance of spectacle—and of nonverbal sound effects—in Western drama.

Spectacle as a Subordinate Factor

Language predominated in Elizabethan theater. Shakespeare worked with a relatively simple uncurtained stage that had an additional upper level. The actors' dialogue would quickly explain the setting for the audience. Thus, early in *Othello*, Shakespeare has Roderigo say:

> Here is her father's house. I'll call aloud.

When the Elizabethan actor did just that, Brabantio would appear on the upper level which, the audience would understand, was a balcony of his residence. But in *The Tempest*, the upper stage was explained as the crow's-nest of a ship.

Whatever additional spectacle the audience might enjoy had to be provided in props that the actors could carry on and off stage, or in special tableaux. Thus Desdemona drops a handkerchief that is picked up by Emilia. There is a great display of "bright swords" when Brabantio's party challenges Othello as a "thief!" And Othello, in his deliberate staging of his own death, provides a spectacular tableau as he stabs himself so he can lean over Desdemona and die on a kiss.

You are alert, then, when you write a report on a play written for such simple spectacle, to this question: How well does the playwright set the stage using mainly words and portable props?

By the time Chekhov is writing, stage managers use a curtain behind which they can set up elaborate spectacle and even change it between acts. This gives us, in *The Cherry Orchard*, a change from a nursery to a meadow to a ballroom.

But aside from establishing the setting as the environment of landed gentry, spectacle still plays a minor role, literally a background role. Lopakin's rich coat and shoes do become "spectacular" when we hear he was born a peasant. And the nursery does take on a kind of symbolic significance in Act IV when Chekhov returns to the setting of Act I. But language still predominates in Chekhov.

Other playwrights like Synge and Rostand were beginning to use spectacle for special effects. In *Riders to the Sea,* the neighbors carry onto stage a dripping canvas sail containing a drowned man. Some reviewers called this cheap and sensational. They still expected drama to be politely literary in its emphasis. And Rostand took a bold step when, in *The Romancers,* he divided his stage with a high wall that serves not only as a realistic setting but also as a symbol of the psychological predicaments of the lovers. Symbolism becomes allegory when the fathers agree at the end to take down the wall separating their families so they may now occupy one undivided site.

Spectacle as a Coordinate Factor

But in Synge and Rostand, spectacle is still mainly an illustration of the language. In the most recent drama, however, spectacle can "say" many things on its own, things essential to the overall meaning which are not stated in any other way. With writers like Samuel Beckett, setting, props, tableau, pantomime, visual symbolism of all kinds become coordinate with verbal statement.

"Godot": Setting

Beckett sets *Godot* with just a road and a tree, both of which become symbolic. The road is the realm of the frenetically active Pozzo and Lucky, while the tree is the locus of the despairing, passive Didi and Gogo. Is the road also to be associated with the Road to Emmaus (Gospel according to Luke, Chapter 24) on which two disciples failed to recognize Jesus? Has Godot appeared without the tramps' recognizing him? Does the single tree suggest the Tree of Knowledge of Good and Evil? Jesus was crucified on crossed tree beams, and so were two thieves. Didi talks a great deal about such matters, and the tramps, who identify with Christ, think of using the tree for their own death. And when it blooms, it sprouts only "four or five" leaves, telling us that in the world of Didi and Gogo, spring is not spectacularly different from winter. Even the stage lighting is symbolic. As soon as the tramps lose all hope that Godot will come today, night falls. Light is hope; darkness is postponement.

Beckett also takes pains to remind his audience that this is a play set in a theater. When Didi needs to urinate, Gogo directs him to the men's room in the theater itself! Setting then helps Beckett make his point that drama is not separate from life: Beckett does *not* try to achieve a "willing suspension of disbelief," does not transport us away from ourselves.

"Godot": Props and Costumes

We have already noted how Didi and Gogo are initially characterized by their concern, respectively, with hat and boots. Their continual search for secondhand clothing also comes to symbolize their trying out new identities. Pozzo's clothing, by contrast, immediately sets him apart as economically successful; his coat is carried by a slave. His watch becomes a major symbol as time becomes a major theme. The leash with which he controls Lucky indicates not only Lucky's slavery but that the slavemaster is also tied, dependent on his slave.

"Godot": Pantomime and Routine

Several of Beckett's main points are delivered initially or even totally through silent dramatic movement. That modern man, in the routine of his life, has become a virtual automaton is dramatized in the way Lucky moves only on command. That "habit is the great deadener" of the mind is made clear first by the calisthenics and boring games in which the tramps routinely engage themselves. Man's condition, whether he is active or passive, is symbolized when all four characters fall and cannot get up.

In other words, in Beckett, spectacle contributes just as much as language does to the overall meaning.

Sound Effects on Stage

In modern drama, sound effects have also taken on greater importance. In *Riders to the Sea*, the splashing of water from the canvas shroud brings Ocean the Antagonist right inside the cottage. In *Godot*, the snapping of Pozzo's whip as he drives Lucky on tells an inhuman story that words could not relate. In *The Cherry Orchard*, two major sounds figure in the meaning. In the final minutes of Act IV we begin hearing "the muffled sound of an axe hitting a tree, a mournful, solitary sound." But as early as Act II "a distant sound is heard, apparently coming from the sky, the sound of a string snapping." The characters wonder, is it the sound of a bucket falling in a pit? of a heron? an owl? This sound effect does more than any spoken word to create an ominous mood. At the end of the play the celestial string snapping interrupts just briefly the sound of the axe in the orchard.

The axe, the whip, and the water dripping are all realistic sounds that take on symbolic meaning. But the mysterious sound heard twice in *The Cherry Orchard* is pure symbolism.

Spectacle and Sound on the Screen

Because he wrote for an audience of 15,000 spread out over a hillside, Sophocles did not try to focus attention on any small artifact or movement. But the movie and TV cameras now give the dramatic writer infinite flexibility of perspective. He can pull back to show planes far apart in the sky, or zoom in for a closeup to catch a tiny tear between the eye and the nose. Since he can record and replay sound as well as sight, he is unlimited in the sound effects he can achieve.

Consider how the opening scenes of *The Mother* communicate a great deal of exposition with absolutely no use of language.

As the image on the TV screen clarifies, we see a quick series of views of New York streets whipped by rain. The big outdoor vista dissolves to the full face of an elderly woman staring through a rain-washed window. Our view widens to include the room behind her: unmade bed, photographs on the wall of children and young adults, and an alarm clock—an old-fashioned circular wind-up clock —which rings at 6:30. We see the old woman's hand drop to turn it off.

We cut to a new scene. Another clock, a modern, streamlined, electric clock goes off at 6:30, not with a ring but with a buzz. A young woman's hand reaches out to cut it off. Our view widens: We are in the bedroom of a young couple.

Before the young man speaks, we have already assimilated worlds of information without having heard a word. Spectacle and nonverbal sound effects have taken their place as coordinates of language. "Total Theater" engages not just the word-hearing mind, it engages the total being.

Evaluating Nonverbal Effects

You are now armed with key information that allows you to pose the crucial questions about your playwright's use of nonverbal effects.

☆ Is the *setting* only described by the characters, and thus suggested to our imagination, as in a Shakespeare production, or is it physically present, as in a Chekhov play?

☆ How much of the *mood* is achieved through *spectacle*? through *sound effects*?

☆ Do any part of the *scenery*, any *props, costumes,* or other parts of the spectacle, or any *sound effects*, take on any *symbolic significance*? Why?

☆ Does the dramatist, in his grouping of the characters, achieve any striking *tableaux*? What do they communicate?

☆ Does the playwright use spectacle as an adjunct, an illustration of language? Or does he/she use spectacle to make statements on its own?

☆ How much do spectacle and sound effects contribute to the *theme*?

Theme and Total Effect

Two contrasting alarm clocks, one old-fashioned and the other modernistic, can signal a theme of conflict between generations.

A sound like a string snapping in the sky can symbolize the end of an era.

A servant can tell us the hero is "ignorant as dirt."

A king who decreed dishonor to the newly dead admits he was wrong. The girl who refused to obey the king's decree is, by implication, declared right.

Action without a crescendo climax may suggest that tragedy can develop in agonizing slowness or in failure to change.

You must, in other words, search for the themes, the overall meaning, of a play in all its components: in the plot, the changes of character, the language, the spectacle, and the sound effects. A theme may be stated explicitly, as when Didi says . . .

Habit is the great deadener

. . . or it may be implied, as when Didi and Gogo do the same pointless things again and again. The chances are that the themes will be stated in several ways, each reinforcing the others.

In trying to formulate the exact themes of your specific play, you can keep in mind that all drama ultimately deals with certain *universal themes*. Once you identify the universal themes, you can restate them in the particular terms of your play. For example, all drama must be concerned, at least in part, with the difference between *illusion* and *reality*. All *characters* differ in the ways their own personal illusions cloud their vision of reality. And *plot* is, after all, nothing but a series of efforts to close the gap between partial knowledge and full truth.

Looking back over the plays we have examined, you can see that playwrights return again and again to variations on this "series of efforts." Always their characters struggle for answers to the great value questions. We can list some of them here and indicate those plays in which the characters search for the answers.

Value Questions	Plays Seeking Answers
Why do men suffer?	*Waiting for Godot* *Othello* *The Mother* *The Cherry Orchard* *Riders to the Sea*
What is the nature of love?	*The Romancers* *Othello* *The Bear*
What is the relation between good and evil?	*Antigone* *Othello* *Waiting for Godot* *The Fall of the City*
What is the proper relation between the individual and society?	*Antigone* *The Fall of the City* *Waiting for Godot* *The Mother*
What is the proper relation between generations?	*The Romancers* *The Mother* *Antigone*
What is the meaning of life?	*Waiting for Godot* *The Mother* *The Cherry Orchard*

You can see now that there are several reliable steps to take in formulating the theme(s) of a play. First you identify the problem that the main characters face. Then summarize their experience in facing this problem. What have they learned about man's condition? Now check your results against our list of great value questions. Does that help? From these reflections you should be able to write a statement about the total meaning of a play.

And, of course, what is *your* reaction to the "total effect"? What do *you* think of both the final message and the author's methods and success in getting it across?

Chapter 4

How to Analyze and Evaluate Poetry

Mood
Music
Metaphor and Meaning

HOW TO ANALYZE AND EVALUATE POETRY

You might find that poetry is the hardest—*or the easiest*—type of literature to write book reports about. And it could depend on you. Why? A few of the reasons:

Poetry appeals largely to your intuition, your imagination, your impulses. Since it is so subjective in its appeal, you are much freer to consider your own personal responses as valid. And it's in the very nature of poetry that your personal responses very likely *will* be relevant.

On the other hand, poetry is the most technical, most artistic of the literary arts. Hence it has developed a vast critical vocabulary. This could confuse and discourage you, and make your task seem harder. Actually, you can make this aspect of poetry appreciation much easier too. You need only remember what we said in the beginning: You can assume the role of the "common reader" writing a layperson's *impressionistic report*; you are *not* an expert, *not* writing an *authoritative review*.

But you might still discover, in this chapter, that you *can* discuss poetic technique without recourse to the highly technical vocabulary by *simply naively describing* (rather than expertly naming) *what is there*. A simple example: Suppose you want to show how Shakespeare's verse contributes to the overall impact of *Othello*. You might analyze a passage we have already discussed:

> One *Mi*chael *Cas*sio, a *Flor*entine,
> (A *fel*low *al*most *damned* in a *fair wife*),
> That *nev*er *set* a *squa*dron *in* the *field*,
> *Nor* the di*vi*sion *of* a *bat*tle *knows* . . .

You could say simply that Shakespeare uses a fairly regular pattern of ten syllables to the line, with five syllables accented, five unaccented. That would do if need be. But if you happen to know that this is decasyllabic verse, with five iambs to the line—that is, iambic pentameter—and that when it is unrhymed, iambic pentameter is called *blank verse*, then you're verging toward a more technical, but not necessarily better, report.

You can gain confidence in analyzing poetry by going from the subjective to the objective. You can start with the *mood* that it creates in you, even before you understand its meaning. Then you can analyze its *music*, the main component of its mood, all the while getting a better idea of the message. Then you can analyze *metaphor and diction*, which bring you to a crossover point, for metaphor has emotional as well as factual meaning and diction is getting closer now to the literal sense. Finally, you can examine the explicit message—in the larger context of *mood*, *music*, and *metaphor*—and attempt some paraphrase of *meaning*. So remember the four M's, and how it's easier to consider them in this order: Mood, Music, Metaphor and diction, Meaning.

Mood

Let's notice first how easy it is to establish mood if you just trust your own naive reactions. We can begin with the opening passage of Alexander Pope's *Essay on Man* (1733–34):

> Awake, my St. John! leave all meaner things
> To low ambition, and the pride of Kings.
> Let us (since Life can little more supply
> Than just to look about us and to die)
> Expatiate free o'er all this scene of Man;
> A mighty maze but not without a plan;
> A Wild, where weeds and flow'rs promiscuous shoot;
> Or Garden, tempting with forbidden fruit.
> Together let us beat this ample field,
> Try what the open, what the covert yield;
> The latent tracts, the giddy heights, explore
> Of all who blindly creep, or sightless soar;
> Eye Nature's walks, shoot Folly as it flies,
> And catch the Manners living as they rise;
> Laugh where we must, be candid where we can;
> But vindicate the ways of God to man.

You refuse to worry at this point about such details as "Who is St. John?" and exactly what Pope means by "Manners." Rather you absorb overall mood. It's not a highly emotional one, certainly. There's excitement, but it's intellectual excitement. There's response to a challenge as the speaker asks someone to join him in a philosophical quest, the purpose of which is clearly stated in the last line. On further readings you can notice how much of this mood is communicated through music, symbol, and choice of words, but first you relax into a working formulation: The poem is animated with *excitement over ideas of great magnitude*.

To see how poets and poems can vary in mood, let's look at the opening *strophe* (verse paragraph) of Samuel Taylor Coleridge's "Kubla Khan" (1816):

> In Xanadu did Kubla Khan
> A stately pleasure-dome decree;
> Where Alph, the sacred river, ran
> Through caverns measureless to man
>   Down to a sunless sea.
> So twice five miles of fertile ground
> With walls and towers were girdled round;
> And here were gardens bright with sinuous rills
> Where blossomed many an incense-bearing tree;
> And here were forests ancient as the hills,
> Enfolding sunny spots of greenery.

Whereas Pope is mainly trying to excite your mind, Coleridge is clearly trying to *excite your senses, emotions, imagination as well as intellect*. Here the overall mood you may feel is one of awe, wonderment, magic, of an atmosphere strange and exotic. If you relax, accept the mystery, not worry too much about literal meanings, you feel a strong tug on your unconscious. You must remind yourself to let the symbols, the sounds, the strangeness all work on you subliminally at first.

But you know that these deepest stirrings will later surface with some explicit message that you can then state as a theme.

What mood does Walt Whitman evoke in you with the opening strophes of his *Song of Myself* (1855–1881)?

> I celebrate myself, and sing myself,
> And what I assume you shall assume,
> For every atom belonging to me as good belongs to you.
>
> I loafe and invite my soul,
> I lean and loafe at my ease observing a spear of summer grass.
>
> My tongue, every atom of my blood, form'd from this soil, this air,
> Born here of parents born here from parents the same, and their
>   parents the same,
> I, now thirty-seven years old in perfect health begin,
> Hoping to cease not till death.
>
> Creeds and schools in abeyance,
> Retiring back a while sufficed at what they are, but never forgotten,
> I harbor for good or bad, I permit to speak at every hazard,
> Nature without check with original energy.

You may respond first to the speaker's *attitude*, which is one of *exuberant self-confidence*, seemingly so because his *self* immediately includes yours as well as his. He invites you to be personal, open, as he intends to be, and to proceed casually by free association, inviting you to entertain notions just as they happen to occur to him/you. Do you feel as though you were breathing a sudden blast of fresh air?

Before we try to explain Pope's excitement of ideas, Coleridge's evocation of wonderment, or Whitman's glorification of us in terms of their music and language, let's include a contemporary poem in our study of various moods poets can create. Here are the opening strophes of Walter James Miller's "Z: In Memory of Louis Zukofsky," which won the Charles Angoff Award after it appeared in *The Literary Review* (Fall 1982).

> Baking a grateful face in a blue and gold day in the Appalachians,
> I'm lazing on a lawn listening like a well-fed cat ears back to the
>   suasions of cicadas.
> At peace even with cyclists snarling up the hill with jets lumbering
>   toward a landing,
> I'm lazing like him who when he loafed invited his soul and by God
>   got RSVPs.
>
> You and I Lou Lou and I suffered under that same fluted dome
>   that *Eagle* dome
> Under which Walt huffed out his editorials under which you
>   and I
> Taught his yawp to engineering majors who suspected all of us
> Of some hoax some humbug passed on from Homer to Horace
>   to Herrick to him and you and me
> But horrors not to them: the class it seemed sat damlike against
>   any chance of seepage

Has the poet succeeded in communicating to you, with music and metaphor as well as with diction, a *warm, quiet restfulness that induces memories and suspense about the meaning of those memories?* Do you see the value of keeping your expression of *mood* as general as possible until you can relate it more specifically to music, symbol, and message?

Music

Before we see how each of these poets has used music to achieve mood and meaning, let us look briefly at the options he had to choose from. Each poet decides on a definite *prosody* to use in each (or many or all) of his poems. His *prosody* is the combination of *stress patterns* and *tonal patterns* he employs. Your first questions, when you analyze prosody, are: Does the poet use a *fixed stress pattern*, called a *meter*, or does he use *free verse*? Or some pattern in between? If fixed meter, which meter?

Fixed Meters

In using a fixed metrical pattern, the poet first decides on his basic *foot*. Usually a foot consists of one accented syllable with a fixed number of un-stressed syllables. There are five basic feet in English prosody. They are:

1. *Iamb,* one unstressed syllable rising to a stressed one, as in each foot of Shakespeare's line:
   > You *blocks,/* you *stones,/* you *worse/* than *sense/* less *things/*

2. *Trochee,* one stress falling to an unaccented syllable, as in each foot of Shakespeare's line:
   > *Double,/ double,/ toil* and*/ trouble/*

3. *Anapest,* two unstressed syllables rising to a stressed one, as in each foot of William Cowper's line:
   > And the *whis/* pering *sound/* of the *cool/* colon*nade/*

4. *Dactyl,* one stressed syllable falling to two unaccented ones, as in the first four feet of T.S. Eliot's line:
   > *Gol*den Oc*/ to*ber de*/ clines* into*/ som*bre No*/ vem*ber/

Another common foot is a two-syllable foot used in place of any of these first four feet, either at random or in a fixed place in the line. This is:

5. *Spondee,* two successive stresses, as used at the end of Longfellow's otherwise dactylic line:
   > *This* is the*/ forest* pri*/ me*val, the*/ murmuring/ pines* and the*/ hem lock/*

In using a fixed metrical pattern, the poet also decides on the number of feet to use per line, and we describe his line then by the type and number of feet it contains. Shakespeare's trochaic line above (*Double, double*) contains four feet; we call it *trochaic tetrameter* (Greek: *tetra,* four; *metron,* measure). Cowper's line is thus called *anapestic tetrameter.* Shakespeare's iambic line (You *blocks*), with five feet, is *iambic pentameter* (*penta,* five). Longfellow's line, with six feet, mainly dactyls, is *dactylic hexameter* (*hexa*, six). A line of one foot would be *monometer*; two, *dimeter*; three, *trimeter*; seven, *heptameter*; eight, *octameter*; nine, *nonameter*.

Meter and Rhythm

Once he establishes his *definite meter*—a line with a fixed number of similar feet—the poet can now achieve musical tension by varying his *rhythms* within that line and even by varying the metrical pattern itself. Notice that in the lines quoted from *Othello* we have both types of variation:

> One Michael Cassio, a Florentine,
> (A fellow almost damned in a fair wife),
> That never set a squadron in the field
> Nor the division of a battle knows . . .

The first line differs in its rhythm from the others. The first line has two pauses, one within the line (called a *caesura*) and one at the end. But the other lines pause only at the end. By varying the *pattern of pauses*, the poet avoids monotonous rhythm. But notice that these lines vary in their meter too:

> One *Mi*/ chael *Cass*/ io,/ a *Flo*/ rentine/

is perfectly regular iambic pentameter. Using the conventional marks for scanning English verse, (–) for an unstressed syllable and (') for a stress, we can mark it thus:

> –　　'/–　　　'/–'/–　'/–　　'/

Then see how the next line varies the meter:

> (A *fell*/ low *all*/ most *damned*/ in a/*fair wife*/)

The last two feet break the pattern:

> –　'/–　　'/–　　　　'/–　–/ '　　'/

Then the third line reasserts the pattern:

> That *ne*/ ver *set*/ a *squad*/ ron in/ the *field*/
> –　　'/–　　'/–　'/–　'/　　'/

And the fourth line varies it again, opening not with an iamb but a trochee:

> *Nor* the/ divi/ sion of/ a bat/ tle knows/
> –/–　'/–　　'/–　'/–　　'/

Loose Metrics

There are two ways a poet can loosen metric verse, making it more flexible. He can use a regular foot but a different *number* of feet in each line. Thus John

Milton, in a choral passage in *Samson Agonistes* (1671), establishes a regular iambic pentameter line:

> But *who*/ is *this,*/ what *thing*/ of *Sea*/ or *Land?*/

And then proceeds to shorten and vary it:

> *Female*/ of *sex*/ it *seems*/
> That *so*/ bedeckt,/ ornate,/ and *gay*/
> *Comes* this *way*/ sailing/
> Like a/ stately/ ship

Notice how, by marking the stresses *and* phrasings of these five lines, we can indicate variations in both meter and rhythm:

```
_ ' _ '        _ ' _ ' _ '
_ ' _ ' _ '
_ ' _ '        _ '        _ '
' _ _ ' _
' _ ' _ '
```

The second way a poet can loosen metric verse is to follow the Old English pattern. This calls for four feet to the line, each foot with one stress but any suitable number of unaccented syllables. Notice the several variations achieved in just two lines from the Anglo-Saxon poem "The Wanderer" (as translated by Stith Thompson):

> Often the *lonely* one   *longs* for *hon*ors
> The *grace* of *God,*   though, *grieved* in his *soul*

```
' _ _   ' _ _        ' _ ' _
_ '   _ '              _ ' _ _ '
```

While the poet achieves metric unity by using four dominant beats, he is actually able to vary each foot, in effect using (in this order) the dactyl ('--), the trochee ('-), the iamb (-'), and an anapest (--'), all in two lines. A version of this kind of loose meters was used by the nineteenth-century Jesuit poet, Father Gerard Manley Hopkins, who called it "sprung rhythm."

Free Verse

When a poet composes in *fixed meters,* he works with lines that contain the same number of similar feet. When he works in *loose metrics,* he composes lines that contain *either* a varying number of similar feet or the same number of dissimilar feet.

But he has a fourth option. He can work in *free verse.* He abandons metrics, with its counting of stresses and its basic unit of the foot. Instead he achieves his forward movement by working with larger units. He works with *word clusters,* balancing words against words, phrases with phrases, clauses with clauses, sometimes in strict parallel structure, repeating key words and phrases that link one line to another. Thus Whitman begins his famous section 32 of *Song of Myself*:

I think I could turn and live with animals, they are so placid
    and self-contain'd,
I stand and look at them long and long.

They do not sweat and whine about their condition,
They do not lie awake in the dark and weep for their sins,
They do not make me sick discussing their duty to God,
Not one is dissatisfied, not one is demented with the mania
    of owning things,
Not one kneels to another, nor to his kind that lived
    thousands of years ago,
Not one is respectable or unhappy over the whole earth.

Contrary to popular belief, good free verse is far more difficult to compose than metric verse. The free verse poet cannot create tensions by using his own rhythms against a standard meter. He has to create tensions by using some of his own rhythms against *other* of his *own* rhythms! As we shall soon see, he might actually have to use richer *tone patterns* than the metricist does in order to achieve comparable musical intensity.

Tonal Patterns

So far we have been concerned with the way a poet achieves music by creating *movement* with words, with flowing contours of rising and falling syllables. Now let's see how a poet colors in those contours with tones. We can analyze his *tonal qualities* by examining the ways he matches vowels and consonants.

Full Rhyme

We say a poet uses a full rhyme when he matches the concluding sounds of two words or phrases. Matching begins with an accented syllable and includes any syllables that may follow. Thus, in Miller's *Making an Angel* (1977) we read:

> She's in her *latency*,
> Which means we have to *wait and see.*

Usually full rhyme occurs at the end of a line, but it can appear within a line too, as in another line from *Making an Angel*:

> You could not *stare* into my comet *glare*

Half Rhymes

The full rhyme matches *both* vowels *and* consonants *and* at least one stressed syllable. But the poet can employ three kinds of *half rhyme*. He can match only the *vowel sounds* in his rhyming words, as in these *Angel* lines:

> Shovel snowdrifts
> Stamped
> "Insufficient postage"

Or she can match only *consonants*, as Emily Dickinson does in these lines:

> 'Twas later when the summer went
> Than when the cricket came
> And yet we knew that gentle clock
> Meant nought but going home

The half rhyme of vowels, as in sn*o*wdrifts–p*o*stage, is called *assonance*; half rhyme of consonants, as in ca*me*–ho*me*, is called *dissonance* or *consonance*. The third kind of half rhyme occurs when the poet matches only unstressed syllables, as in this *Angel* couplet:

> Stamps not pasted in the upp*er*
> Right-hand corn*er*

Alliteration

Instead of concentrating on matching sounds at the ends of words, the poet can match sounds at the beginning. This is *alliteration* or *initial rhyme,* and you have seen it in our Anglo-Saxon quotation:

> Often the *l*onely one   *l*ongs for honors
> The *g*race of *G*od,   though, *g*rieved in his soul

In initial rhyme, any initial stressed vowel is assumed to alliterate with any other initial stressed vowel, so that this line from the same poem is also considered alliterative:

> *O*ften alone   at *e*arly dawn

Onomatopoeia

An important tonal effect poets often aim at involves use of words whose sounds resemble or suggest their meaning. When you read lines like these from Tennyson's *The Princess* (1847)

> The *moan* of doves in *immemorial* elms,
> And *murmuring* of *innumerable* bees

you are reading *onomatopoetic* lines. They contain words that imitate the sounds they describe.

Strophes and Stanzas

As soon as the poet carries his stresses and tones beyond one line, he is concerned with building the major unit of his work: the equivalent in poetry of the paragraph in prose. The all-inclusive term for any verse paragraph is *strophe*. But if all the strophes in a poem have the same structure, we prefer to call them *stanzas*. And so the word *strophes* tends to be used mainly for successive verse paragraphs with varying structures. You can see that Dickinson's poem

> 'Twas later when the summer went
> Than when the cricket came,
> And yet we knew that gentle clock
> Meant nought but going home.

> 'Twas sooner when the cricket went
> Than when the winter came,
> Yet that pathetic pendulum
> Keeps esoteric time.

is organized in *stanzas*. But Whitman's

> I celebrate myself, and sing myself,
> And what I assume you shall assume,
> For every atom belonging to me as good belongs to you.
>
> I loafe and invite my soul,
> I lean and loafe at my ease observing a spear of summer grass.

is organized in *strophes*.

Nomenclature

There are numerous types of standard stanzas used in English poetry, and, of course, an infinite number of possible strophe forms. But once again, remember, you need not know the name for each stanza you write about, you need only be able to describe it accurately. For example, Dickinson's stanza is called a *quatrain*. You could describe it, if need be, as a four-line stanza.

Quatrain

Dickinson's quatrains use alternating four-stress (*tetrameter*) and three-stress (*trimeter*) lines, rhyming only on the shorter lines (*a b c b*). This form of the quatrain is used and known as the *ballad stanza*. But the quatrain can employ lines of any length and a variety of rhyme schemes (*a b a b, a a b a, a b b a*, etc.).

Couplet

Two successive lines of verse tied by rhyme constitute a *couplet*. The lines may be of different length, as in the *latency* couplet, but normally they are of the same meter. Milton uses an *iambic tetrameter couplet* in "L'Allegro" (1632):

> Thus done the tales, to bed they creep,
> By whispering winds soon lulled asleep.

And Pope uses *iambic tetrameter couplets* in his *Essay on Criticism* (1711). Two typical couplets are:

> Some have at first for wits, then poets passed,
> Turned critics next, and proved plain fools at last.
> Some neither can for wits nor poets pass,
> As heavy mules are neither horse nor ass.

By Pope's time, the iambic pentameter line had been established as the *heroic* meter for English, that is, the meter most suitable for epic, narrative, dramatic, and philosophical poetry. Hence the rhymed iambic pentameter couplet is known also as the *heroic couplet*.

You can see, from portions of Pope so far sampled, that he preferred the *closed couplet*, a major mode of poetic expression in the neoclassical age. In the closed couplet, there is usually a pause at the end of the first line and the rounding out of a thought by the end of the second. Content, in other words, is tailored to the ten-syllable line, and most lines are *end-stopped*.

By contrast, we have the *open couplet,* in which meaning can spill over from one line to another in what we call *run-on lines* (or, using the French, *enjambement*). Lord Byron, a Romantic in rebellion against the closed couplet, thus dramatized his preference for the open form:

> I say no more than hath been said in Dante's
> Verse, and by Solomon and by Cervantes.

The run-on quality can best be appreciated in Romantic works like John Keats' *Endymion* (1817–18):

> A thing of beauty is a joy forever:
> Its loveliness increases, it will never
> Pass into nothingness; but will keep
> A bower quiet for us, and a sleep
> Full of sweet dreams, and health, and quiet breathing. . .

Shakespeare, as we saw in our study of drama, uses the heroic couplet for special effects, including ending a scene:

> *Iago.*   I have't! It is engend'red! Hell and night
> Must bring this monstrous birth to the world's light.

Heroic Blank Verse

But for the greater portion of his plays, Shakespeare uses unrhymed iambic pentameter, usually called *blank verse,* although here too the adjective *heroic* has been applied. As we can see from Othello's final speech, Shakespeare uses both *end-stopped* and *run-on blank verse:*

> Soft you! a word or two before you go.
> I have done the state some service, and they know't—
> No more of that. I pray you, in your letters,
> When you shall these unlucky deeds relate,
> Speak of me as I am. Nothing extenuate,
> Nor set down aught in malice. Then must you speak
> Of one that loved not wisely, but too well . . .

Blank verse has been a dominant poetic form in English poetry, used by major poets from Christopher Marlowe to James Merrill.

Rime Royal

Geoffrey Chaucer enjoyed special success when grouping seven iambic pentameter lines, rhymed *a b a b b c c,* to form the stanza known as *rime royal.* His verse novel *Troilus and Criseyde* is a good example of sustained use of this stanza.

Ottava Rima

When poets group eight iambic pentameter lines in a rhyme scheme of *a b a b a b c c,* we call the result *ottava rima.* Ariosto and Tasso chose this stanza for epic poetry, and Lord Byron used it in *Don Juan.*

Spenserian Stanza

For his *Faerie Queene,* Edmund Spenser invented a special stanza, since used by many poets including Byron, Shelley, and Keats. It comprises two iambic pentameter quatrains followed by one iambic hexameter, all interlinked by a scheme of *a b a b b c b c c.*

Sonnet

A verse form comprised of fourteen iambic pentameter lines is the *sonnet*. It seems to constitute a one-stanza poem. Actually, in either its Italian or its English rhyme scheme, the sonnet is a combination of stanzaic forms. And since sonnets are often composed in sequences, each sonnet then becomes one unit, in effect, one stanza. The Italian sonnet is composed of two parts: an *octave* or eight-line section, usually rhymed *a b b a a b b a*, and a *sestet*, or six-liner, rhymed *c d c d c d*, or *c d e c d e*, or some other way. English poets successful with the Italian form are Thomas Wyatt, Milton, William Wordsworth, and Keats. The English sonnet is composed of three successive *quatrains* followed by a *couplet*, typically rhyming *a b a b, c d c d, e f e f, g g*. Invented by Henry Surrey, the English form reached its peak performances in Shakespeare's sequence, and so this form is often called the Shakespearean sonnet.

Identifying Poetic Paragraphs

You have probably figured out by now how to identify and describe the type of verse paragraph, or strophe, that a poet is using in any particular work. First, you count the number of lines in each paragraph. If the number differs in each case, then you say that the poem is composed of *irregular strophes*. If the number of lines is the same in each strophe, you know the poem is composed in regular strophes called *stanzas*. The number of lines in a stanza, and the rhyme scheme, can help you identify each type: two rhymed lines, a *couplet*; four, a *quatrain*; six, a *sestet*; and so on. If you cannot identify the exact name of the stanzaic form—we can't discuss them all here, and anyhow, poets often invent their own stanzas—then you simply *describe* the stanza structure.

But keep in mind that, whether you name or simply describe a poet's strophic unit, your purpose is to evaluate its effectiveness as a musical medium for his message.

Analyzing Music: *Essay on Man*

You can practice on the poems we have read for *mood*. You glance down the ends of the lines of *Essay on Man*, for example:

> Awake, my St. John!   leave all meaner things
> To low ambition and the pride of Kings.
> Let us, since life can little more supply
> Than just to look about us and to die,
> Expatiate free o'er all this scene of Man;
> A mighty maze! but not without a plan . . .

And from the pattern of the *end rhymes*, you know the basic form is the *rhymed couplet*. Then you count the syllables in several lines and scan their accents, unstressed syllables, caesuras, and pauses, like this:

```
_' _''      '_'_'
_'_'_'_'
_'      _'_'_'
_'_'_'_'
_'_'_'_'
_'_'      _'_'_'
```

And now you can say that these are *iambic pentameter (heroic) couplets*. And you can show how Pope both establishes the standard meter for such a couplet . . .

> To low ambition and the pride of Kings.

. . . and creates rhythmic tensions within that meter in two ways: In some lines, he pauses only once, at the end; in others, he pauses at some variable point within the line as well. He indicates his intention of varying the meter itself in his very first verse. And his very first couplet is a *closed couplet,* expressing a complete idea in 20 syllables, establishing the ideal form for the rest of the poem.

You ask next: Is there *inner music* as well as *end rhyme*? You discover that *alliteration* abounds, propelling words toward each other: *l*eave, *l*ow, *l*et, *l*ife, *l*ittle, *l*ook; *m*y, *m*eaner, *m*ore, *m*ighty *m*aze. And the full rhyme of supply–die is echoed in *assonant rhymes*: pride, life, mighty. Two lines have inner links in emphatic *assonance*: leave–meaner, free–scene.

You are ready to explain how Pope's music has helped set up the mood. The confident march of the meter, abrupt surprises in rhythm, bright tones, the neat and efficient way that ideas are tailored, all help to create a sense of intellectual organization, excitement, and promise.

Analyzing Music: "Kubla Khan"

One glance over Coleridge's poem and you see its three sections are greatly dissimilar in both length and shape: It is composed in highly *irregular rhymed strophes.*

> In Xanadu did Kubla Khan
> A stately pleasure dome decree:
> Where Alph, the sacred river, ran
> Through caverns measureless to man
> Down to a sunless sea.
> So twice five miles of fertile ground
> With walls and towers were girdled round:
> And there were gardens bright with sinuous rills,
> Where blossomed many an incense-bearing tree;
> And here were forests ancient as the hills,
> Enfolding sunny spots of greenery.
>
> But oh! that deep romantic chasm which slanted
> Down the green hill athwart a cedarn cover!
> A savage place! as holy and enchanted
> As e'er beneath a waning moon was haunted
> By woman wailing for her demon-lover!
> 'And from this chasm, with ceaseless turmoil seething,
> As if this earth in fast thick pants were breathing,
> A mighty fountain momently was forced:
> Amid whose swift half-intermitted burst
> Huge fragments vaulted like rebounding hail,
> Or chaffy grain beneath the thresher's flail:

And 'mid these dancing rocks at once and ever
It flung up momently the sacred river.
Five miles meandering with a mazy motion
Through wood and dale the sacred river ran,
Then reached the caverns measureless to man,
And sank in tumult to a lifeless ocean:
And 'mid this tumult Kubla heard from far
Ancestral voices prophesying war!
   The shadow of the dome of pleasure
   Floated midway on the waves;
   Where was heard the mingled measure
   From the fountain and the caves.
It was a miracle of rare device,
A sunny pleasure-dome with caves of ice!

   A damsel with a dulcimer
   In a vision once I saw:
   It was an Abyssinian maid,
   And on her dulcimer she played,
   Singing of Mount Abora.
   Could I revive within me
   Her symphony and song,
   To such a deep delight 'twould win me,
That with music loud and long,
I would build that dome in air,
That sunny dome! those caves of ice!
And all who heard should see them there,
And all should cry, Beware! Beware!
His flashing eyes, his floating hair!
Weave a circle round him thrice,
And close your eyes with holy dread,
For he on honey-dew hath fed,
And drunk the milk of Paradise.

The dominant meter is *iambic*, shifting often to *trochaic* or even *dactylic*, and many lines contain either an extra syllable or one less than we would expect. The lines range from a short trimeter of six syllables

Down to a sunless sea

to a burst of long meters up to 11 or 12 syllables

And from this chasm, with ceaseless turmoil seething

The rhyme follows no set pattern and is full of surprises. The opening strophe, for example, consists of a five-line section rhymed *a b a a b*, followed by a closed couplet *c c*, ending with a quatrain rhymed *d b d b*. The *shifting rhyme patterns* and very *loose metrics* mean that matching sounds occur at highly unpredictable intervals.

Coleridge's *inner music* is equally rich. Like all great poems, this one seems built on full open vowels: As we read it aloud, we are obliged to keep our mouth open to form one round sound after another. The very first line makes full use of open *a* and *u* sounds . . .

> In X*a*n*a*d*u* did K*u*bla Khan . . .

that will echo through the poem in wonderful series like

> rom*a*ntic ch*a*sm which sl*a*nted

and

> mid this t*u*m*u*lt K*u*bla

Consonants too are enhanced with frequent *alliteration*.

> Five *m*iles *m*eandering with a *m*azy *m*otion . . .

> A *d*amsel with a *d*ulcimer . . .

Coleridge's music, in short, generates an excitement quite different from Pope's. Pope's excites us about an ordered, understood, rational world. Coleridge's excites us about a turbulent, mysterious, wondrously dynamic world.

Analyzing Music: *Song of Myself*

Even though you see at a glance that Whitman's poetry is nonmetric, cast in free verse strophes, you will find it valuable to scan his lines:

> I celebrate myself, and sing myself,
> And what I assume you shall assume,
> For every atom belonging to me as good belongs to you.
>
> I loafe and invite my soul,
> I lean and loafe at my ease observing a spear of summer grass.
>
> My tongue, every atom of my blood, form'd from this soil, this air,
> Born here of parents born here from parents the same, and their
>   parents the same,
> I, now thirty-seven years old in perfect health begin,
> Hoping to cease not till death.
>
> Creeds and schools in abeyance,
> Retiring back a while sufficed at what they are, but never
>   forgotten,
> I harbor for good or bad, I permit to speak at every hazard,
> Nature without check with original energy.

You may then make the amazing discovery that his free verse is actually a combination of *many modes of formal prosody*. His feet are, in actuality, *mainly iambic*:

> Retiring back a while sufficed at what they are . . .

tightening sometimes to a series of *spondees*:

> Born here of parents born here from parents the same,
> ′   ′ – ′ – ′ ′ – ′ – – ′

> and their parents the same,
> – ′ ′ ′ – – ′

> I, now, thirty-seven years old . . .
> ′ ′ ′ – ′ – ′ ′

and relaxing into *dactyls*:

> Nature without check with original energy.
> ′ – – ′ ′ ′ – – ′ – – ′ – –

Scanning also shows you that Whitman makes excellent use of *caesuras* . . .

> I celebrate myself   and sing myself
> And what I assume   you shall assume

. . . so that what we have called a balancing of word clusters is also a rhythm of intervals.

And far from being unmusical because he doesn't use full rhyme, Whitman instead exploits all the resources of internal music. Notice for example the magic matching of key sounds in the opening line:

> I *cel*ebrate my*self*, and sing my*self*

Also notice the *alliteration* throughout, like the four s sounds in the first line and repetitions of *l* and *s* sounds in the fifth line. The alliteration carries along with it other matching sounds:

> My *ton*gue, every a*tom* . . .

And see how the midsection is bodied with *internal assonant rhymes*: form'd, Born, born; parents, their parents; culminating in a double off-rhyme that is both assonant *and* dissonant yet *not* a full rhyme: health, death. And the most magical trick of all is one that could be boring if used by a lesser poet: repetition of words, like I, *myself, assume, belong, loafe*.

You find, then, that Whitman's free verse is the appropriate medium for his mood. For his restlessness, his new democratic American pride, his new sense of freedom and expansiveness, he needs the newest, most flexible rhythms possible. And from his rich heritage of prosody, he needs to use not a narrow set of traditional forms but to draw freely from a broad range of techniques.

Analyzing Music: "Z"

You are now ready to try out your knowledge of prosody on a contemporary poem. What will you look for in the *music*? *Strophic form; metrics; rhymes: full, assonant, dissonant, initial;* and *onomatopoeia*. Notice that "Z" has a superscription intended, like the subtitle, to set the occasion in the reader's mind. You do not count this as part of the poem's structure.

Z:
In Memory of Louis Zukofsky

> *Louis Zukofsky, 74, a Major Poet*
> *Of Objectivist School and Novelist*
> *—The New York Times, May 14, 1978*

Baking a grateful face in a blue and gold day in the Appalachians,
I'm lazing on a lawn listening like a well-fed cat ears back to
      the suasions of cicadas.
At peace even with cyclists snarling up the hill with jets
      lumbering toward a landing,
I'm lazing like him who when he loafed invited his soul and by
      God got RSVPs.

You and I Lou Lou and I suffered under that same fluted dome   5
      that *Eagle* dome
Under which Walt huffed out his editorials under which you
      and I
Taught his yawp to engineering majors who suspected all of us
Of some hoax some humbug passed on from Homer to Horace
      to Herrick to him and you and me
But horrors not to them: the class it seemed sat damlike against
      any chance of seepage

Between classes we stood sullen in the dull hall, smokers   10
Lost in clouds as gray as board erasers at the close of the
      classroom day
Chalkdust on our elbows   ashes on our shoes   absence on our
      faces
Mulling over phrases . . . left unleavened or unbaked
To meet our evening classes . . . to prove there's design in the
      canticles . . . to minds who heard their rapture
In crackling circuits in wind tunnels in bubbling trays of the   15
      column

"I'm waiting to hear from *Botteghe Oscure*," you might say.
      "They used to pay."
Or with the thriftiest movement—you smoked with the shortest
      slowest possible swing
Of hand from hip to lip—you'd pull out onionskins creased
      greasy like old deeds:
"Been working on this one for years." Was it "*A*"? or *Bottom
      on Shakespeare*? Should I have reached for it?
Anyway, something surreptitious: in a world of crackling facts   20
      tunneled wind
Columns of all kinds, the poet working under the rose under a
      sootlined rose

Sometimes you seemed made of pipecleaners   wires twisted to
      hold tufts of absorbent stuff
Or you seemed like pungent nightshade rolled into a cylinder of
      rice paper

Or you stood so black in your beetle brows so weightless
      tentative
That children candid in their game of animals would guess you   25
      a fly
And true in the boring committee you did brood sad-eyed like
      a fly in October

One night in that wallway curtained with gray fuming I pulled
      out
A poem catafalqued in a magazine so obscurer than *Botteghe*
You had never heard of it. "I don't keep up," you murmured
      always diplomatic.
You smoked my poem with all pores open. "Well, they *are*   30
      matronly," you exhaled.
"Yes riverboats are matronly." You stared at them sailing at the
      end of the hall.
"*I hear a cricket scraping its limited instrument.* That's good.
      Know why that's good?"
"Sure!" said Bottom to the Bard. O asshead of course knew all
      about onomatopoeia!
A sudden machete swung in panic had cut down some blue and
      green beginning
Rooted in those ashes. Loose in lugubrious silence sinking back   35
      into the printed page
You looked up once with smoldering pity for someone safe now
      from the greatening of praise

"You're failing her in some way," you'd say later of my ailing
      matehood.
Always—as in your poetry played on a violin fitted with secret
      organ stops—
You sounded only the radius. Meaning the total terrorful   39
      circumference

You spot the strophic form as Whitmanic because the strophes are irregular and unrhymed. Applying your lesson from Whitman, you do some scansion, because any poet—regular metricist or free verse writer—usually establishes his music in his opening lines. You do a full scansion of "Z"'s first strophe, something like this:

```
 ' _ _ ' _ '          _ _ ' _ ' ' _ _ ' _ ' _
_ ' _ ' _ '          ' _ ' _ ' _ '          ' ' ' _ ' _ ' _ '
_ ' ' _ _ ' _ ' _ ' _ '          _ ' ' _ ' _ ' _
_ ' _ _ ' _ ' _ '          _ ' _ _ '          _ _ '          ' ' ' ' '
```

You can now say that the poet employs a line, ranging from 18 to 23 syllables long, that comprises all the basic feet. In the first line alone, you find examples of dactyl, anapest, iamb, trochee, spondee. Yet the number of accents—ranging from 8 to 13 per line—roughly averages out to be one stress for each unstressed syllable: *it averages out to iambic,* so to speak. *This is an important clue to the modern poet's control over his rhythms.* Here they rise from a loose dactylic-anapestic line 1 to a staccato spondee series at the close of the strophe. You can use this discovery to see how lengthening and shortening, loosening and tightening, of the feet corresponds to rise and fall in music and story. In this connection, notice how that author's heavy use of Whitmanic *caesuras* also helps him speed up or slow down the flow of meaning.

The very first line gives you important clues to the poem's tonal qualities. There is *assonant rhyme* in a series of "ay" sounds:

Baking a grateful face in a blue and gold day in the Appalachians

And there is *interlocking alliteration*:

Baking . . . grateful . . . blue . . . gold

These techniques are used throughout, from the assonant lazing– suasions– cicadas of line 2 to the failing– later– ailing matehood– radius of the last strophe; and from the alliterative lazing–lawn–listening like to the poetry played and total terrorful of the final line.

The poet takes pains too to establish *onomatopoeia* in his opening strophe not only for its own sake as music, but because it will play an important part in the narrative experience:

suasions of cicadas

cyclists *snarling*

jets *lumbering* toward a landing

These are all imitations of the sounds they refer to, all preparing us for the climactic moment related to

. . . a cricket *scraping its limited instrument* . . .

Now, unless you can find several other examples of *dissonance* besides dull– hall, you would have to state that this poet uses *consonant half-rhyme* much less frequently than *vowel half-rhyme*.

You have demonstrated, in short, exactly how *stress patterns* and *tone patterns* play a major role in creating the mood and the movement of "Z".

Metaphor and Meaning

You have, let us say, read a poem often enough to be able to "report" on its mood and music. (T.S. Eliot figured on *five* readings before he could be sure of a poem's worth!) You are now ready to examine more closely the poem's language for both its literal and its metaphoric values. After that you will be able to combine mood, music, and metaphor into a full statement of overall meaning. And you will be able to offer, with confidence, your own impression of the "poem's worth"!

Meaning: *Essay on Man*

You get back then, to Pope's "choice of words," the effects of his language . . .

> Awake, my St. John! leave all meaner things
> To low ambition and the pride of Kings.
> Let us, since life can little more supply
> Than just to look about us and to die,
> Expatiate free o'er all this scene of Man;   5
> A mighty maze! but not without a plan;
> A Wild, where weeds and flowers promiscuous shoot,
> Or Garden, tempting with forbidden fruit.
> Together let us beat this ample field,
> Try what the open, what the covert yield;   10
> The latent tracts, the giddy heights, explore
> Of all who blindly creep or sightless soar;
> Eye Nature's walks, shoot Folly as it flies,
> And catch the Manners living as they rise;
> Laugh where we must, be candid where we can,   15
> But vindicate the ways of God to man.

The very first couplet *shocks*. You did not expect *meaner things* and *low ambition* to be linked with *Kings*. In *rousing his friend* (Henry St. John) to realize that their philosophical concerns are far above ambitions for power, Pope is *rousing us too*. *Shocks, surprise, new perspectives* are all accomplished swiftly in compact musical language — these make up the very stuff of poetry. The shocks are repeated in *contrast* after *contrast,* a major mode in the arts (think of contrasting colors in painting, opposing melodies in a symphony). What we think of as a full lifetime is compared/ contrasted with a mere *glance around* our circumstances! No sooner are you made to think of a *mighty maze* than you are forced to reconcile it with a *plan*. Pope is expert in the use of such *paradox*—that is, a statement that seems to contradict itself but contains enough truth to bridge the apparent opposites. *Paradox* is another essential of poetry: All literature seeks the reality behind the appearance.

Next you contrast a Wild with a Garden, and now single words begin to expand into rainbows of meaning. In Pope's day, in the Age of Reason, the garden, well-planned and cared for, was the man-made answer to the seeming "chaos" of Nature. Pope is suggesting that the *scene of man* is not as random or haphazard as a wilderness, but as well-*cultivated,* well thought-out, as any horticultural triumph of the Age of Reason. But Pope's Garden is also related to God's *plan,* to the Edenic Garden with its "forbidden fruit." Pope also uses the Garden as a *symbol* (a thing that stands for something larger than itself, usually something material that represents something immaterial). His Garden becomes the "place," the realm of ideas, where he and St. John can explore such major concerns as Man's nature, his place in the overall scheme, his relation to God.

Then Pope ventures on an extended *metaphor,* a likening of unlike things. He implicitly compares his quest for the meaning of life to a hunting trip. He and St. John will beat the bushes to flush out their prey, "shoot Folly" and Manners (customs, fashions, mores) as they are forced into the open flight of rational analysis. The passage ends with another type of figure of speech, the *allusion*. The line . . .

> But vindicate the ways of God to man.

echoes line 26 of Milton's *Paradise Lost,* where Milton proposes, in his story of Adam and Eve, to

> . . . justifie the wayes of God to men.

Our poet, then, has communicated his meanings *indirectly, suggestively,* through metaphor, and *directly, explicitly* through literal statement. As a poet of ideas, primarily, Pope is always careful to conclude each passage with an explicit message. You would not be surprised, then, to come to the end of Epistle I of *Essay on Man* and find that the message is summed up in a combination of metaphorical, paradoxical, and literal statements, with final emphasis on the bluntly literal, almost *prosaic* truth.

> All Nature is but Art, unknown to thee;
> All Chance, Direction, which thou canst not see;
> All Discord, Harmony, not understood;
> All partial Evil, universal Good:
> And, spite of Pride, in erring Reason's spite,
> One truth is clear, "WHATEVER IS, IS RIGHT."

Meaning: "Kubla Khan"

Even when his words form analogies and echo mythic concepts, Pope is driving for speedy *mental results all readers can agree on.* But as you turn to Coleridge, you find yourself in a totally different kind of poetry. He uses words to stir up our feelings and imagination, to rouse our senses, to suggest, to communicate with our unconscious awareness *before* he addresses our consciousness. He wants the mental aspects of our experience to be slow, gradual, cumulative, with *each reader coming to his own conclusions.*

And that's your cue!

You must, in your book report on poetry like Coleridge's, be confident in your own impressions. Relax and describe your own experience with the poem. In other words, be the naive layperson, the "common reader" that the author aims at ultimately. On the other hand, use whatever specialized knowledge you do have to help you assemble conclusions. Out of such knowledge, you can venture some "authoritative" remarks as well as impressionistic ones. Use the "two-track" approach. And that's what we'll do here.

Impressionistic Analysis

By now you are sure that even structure conveys meaning. "Kubla Khan" has three sections. You see not only some simple allegiance here to the idea of "beginning, middle, end," but to the idea you have studied so well in fiction and drama: Three parts can mean a situation *before* a change, *during* a change, and *after.* Will that work in your analysis of "Kubla Khan"?

The first strophe describes an *ancient, sacred, sunny,* protected place (*girdled round*) where there is a *pleasure dome.* The second is obviously going to describe some kind of change or difference because it opens with *But oh!* We are now not only in a sacred (*holy*) place, but *A savage place!* Here there is *ceaseless turmoil, tumult, war,* passionate love, and the *dome* now has *caves of ice* and it *casts shadows.* We have passed from a safe, sunny, warm scene to one that also includes danger and extreme cold.

The third strophe seems to put the two opposite experiences together. The poet wishes he could *build that dome in air* (a castle in the air, an ideal), so we know that it's a thing of the past now that can be recaptured only in the imagination. But it would be different from the original *sunny dome* of the first strophe because it would include *those caves of ice*. And alas! If the poet could *revive* that dome, people would *Beware* of him with *holy dread* because he would be *drunk* with *milk of Paradise . . . .*

Aha! The last word of strophe three now gives a clue to what was being described in strophe one!

After all, what else could an *ancient, sacred, sunny*, safe, protected place be but a Paradise? Indeed, strophe one does have gardens with *many an incense-bearing tree*. The Garden of *Eden* then? *The* Tree?

If so, then strophe one is a world of innocence, and strophe two would be the world of experience, the world after Eden—after the Fall! A world caused by a *woman wailing for her demon-lover*—Eve for Satan? A post-Edenic world that includes passionate love, as well as *ceaseless turmoil* and *war*. A world in which the poet has lost the power to *build that dome* even *in air*. A world without imagination, where people would *Beware* the poet.

Authoritative Analysis

Now suppose you had done only the simple "feeling your way through" described in the first three paragraphs of our Impressionistic Analysis, down to our quote from *the milk of Paradise*. You would already have enough to write about, wouldn't you? But beginning with the insight into strophe one as Eden, two as the real world thereafter, you were beginning to use more specialized knowledge. Let's see what other kinds of knowledge could be used by you, or someone else in your class, or your teacher.

You wonder why *the sacred river* is named *Alph*. Does it suggest *alpha*, the first letter of the *alphabet*? Certainly fits in with those *ancient* beginnings, reinforcing the idea of *Xanadu* as Eden. Suppose you happen here to know that Alpheus, a river in Greece, was believed in ancient times to go underground and reemerge as a spring—a fountain!

Aha! There's a fountain in strophe two. So our *sacred river* of innocent Eden has gone underground—*Down to a sunless sea*—and emerged in the post-Edenic world as a fountain that runs, again, down *to a lifeless ocean*.

To some people, especially those who know biology, *sunless sea* will connote the *amniotic fluid*, the salty liquid in the womb in which the fetus lives—in its *sunless* world, *girdled round*, protected in the dark! The womb, then, might be that safe Eden at the beginning of time (life). Is it, indeed, the *pleasure dome* that houses the fetus? The poet, indeed all of us, as depth psychologists would tell us, want to return to the womb—that is, to a protected *Paradise*.

Who created the *Paradise* named *Xanadu*? The poet tells us Kubla Khan *decreed* it. In the beginning was the Word. *Kubla* is a God-figure.

Some readers would even bring in *very* highly specialized knowledge like this: One type of *dulcimer*, in the *ancient* world, was the monochord—a one-stringed instrument. It was on a monochord that the Pythagoreans, mathematicians *and* mystics, worked out their discovery of the secrets of the octave, the intervals of the scale. And then they assumed that the universe was built on the same secrets—the harmonious music of the spheres!

So our poet, in his vision, has seen an *Abyssinian maid* playing a *dulcimer* which connotes the secrets of Creation. Why *Abyssinian*? Well, in Ethiopia (formerly Abyssinia), there is a branch of the Nile which long ago was believed to be a kind of Alpheus river, disappearing underground, reemerging elsewhere. Why *Abyssinian*? Is the *Abyss* related to *that deep romantic chasm* from which all this *ceaseless turmoil* is *flung up*?

One final sampling of the thousands of bits of specialized knowledge that *could* figure here: Some books give this poem the subtitle *Kubla Khan: Or, a Vision in a Dream.* Maybe you, and/or your teacher, are familiar with this version which includes Coleridge's account of how he came to write *Kubla Khan.* It came to him in a dream. Did we need that information here? Hardly. Depth psychology tells us that a poem and a dream both come from the same sources in the unconscious. Both would be subject to the same kind of authoritative analysis.

But by now, each reader, with specialized knowledge different in every case, is putting together a different constellation of ideas. Your book report on Coleridge would be different in subject matter from that of each of your classmates. And, of course, it would also differ in interpretation.

Meaning: "I Celebrate Myself"

As you start *Song of Myself,* you realize that like Pope, Whitman relies on a series of surprises and shocks to excite us about his subject matter. But to surprises in content, Whitman adds a new kind of shock. This is the way in which he *links his ideas.*

Pope and most pre-Whitman poets built strong bridges from thought to thought. Whitman is likely to use gaps instead of bridges. As his reader, you yourself must often supply transitions and connections. Whitman gives you the pleasure of participating in the making of relationships. The way he stimulates you to leap the gap, in your own way, is closer to the thought process itself. Thought is a steady flow, but a flow of *separate* images and notions. Pope's poetry is thought reorganized into a logical progression. Whitman's is often raw thought in psychological order, that is, *free association.*

Whitman delivers his first "content" shock in his very first phrase. In our culture, we are *not* supposed to celebrate the self. Whitman proceeds to a second shock, a *paradox*: In celebrating *myself,* I *celebrate you* too, for we are all made of the same atoms. So the "I" that Whitman celebrates is the Romanticist "I." The Romanticist believes that it's valuable for me to delve into *me* because I'll find out more about *us.* Still, Whitman's original point remains clear: In order to carry out this process, each of us *should* glorify the Self.

His second strophe delivers another shock. In our culture, we are not supposed *to loafe* in order to *invite* the *soul.* In a work-ethic society, we are expected to find ourselves, reach virtue, the spirit and salvation through hard labor. Loafing is suspect. In Whitman's day especially, idleness was equated with evil, and today it's still contrary to the notion of "getting ahead." In a rat-race world, people don't *loafe at . . . ease observing a spear of summer grass.* Whitman is seducing us into a different world, where idleness is the key to creation and discovery.

Apparently, it's staring at the *spear of summer grass* that leads him to think that he himself—*every atom of his blood*—is like the grass, *form'd from this soil.* But the links in thinking are not spelled out in the poem as we are spelling them out here. Apparently, when you *loafe* you are better able to take quick, bold leaps in thought, make connections by swift intuition.

So now *he* is not only *you* and *us,* he's also all Nature; in effect, *every atom belonging to me . . . belongs to . . . this soil, this air* as well. This too is a shocking idea. In Whitman's time, and still often in our own time, man sees himself as the *adversary* of Nature. Modern culture is built on Francis Bacon's proposal that we put Nature on the rack and torture her for her secrets! Whitman insists rather that man is blood kin to *grass*, *air*, and *soil*. In this sense, Whitman anticipates the ecology-mindedness of our day. He is prophetic too about his own life. He begins his *Song of Myself*—part of his book *Leaves of Grass*—hoping *to cease not till death*. Starting *Song* and *Leaves* in 1855, he would not complete the final edition until 1881—what we now call the Deathbed Edition.

Again without explicit transition, he leaps to another notion. While he works at this lifetime task, he sees *Creeds and schools in abeyance*, that is, formal systems of belief will be kept in a state of suspension. Indeed, several common beliefs—like the work ethic, the way to evoke the soul, the proper way to proceed from idea to idea—have already been suspended. *In abeyance* also means, in law, unsettled or undetermined. Whitman intends, so long as he lives, to keep his ideas flexible, subject to change, never "finalized."

Apparently then, in order to *celebrate* one*self*, one must be free of preconceptions, old ideas, conventional creeds. Nevertheless, the poet will allow them a hearing, because in his all-inclusiveness, his catholicity, he can deny nothing, he is (like) *Nature without check with original energy*.

The beautiful opening and closing phrases of this final strophe are typical of the kind that earned Whitman the epithet of "great phrase-maker"—the kind you will savor repeatedly as you advance further into the *Song*, taking notes on his phraseology, his free associations, his shocking ideas that put all our smug old notions into a new context.

Meaning: "Z"

You should feel confident now to tackle any contemporary poem, for you have been introduced to virtually all the techniques and devices today's poet has inherited. If you run into anything you don't understand, you will bypass it, as we did in "Kubla Khan," trying first to gain an overview, returning only later to puzzling details.

As you study the language of "Z", you find the poet makes full use of shocking expressions, irony, metaphors, free associations, puns, and allusions, as well as literal statements.

Since you're now familiar with Whitman's "I Celebrate Myself," you'll understand at once the *allusion* the author of "Z" makes in line 4. He shocks us with an unexpected twist to Whitman's idea of sending out such invitations.

Another allusion to Whitman takes on both *literal* and *symbolic meaning*. Whitman was for a while editor of the *Brooklyn Daily Eagle*; the famous *Eagle* building, in Zukofsky's time, was used at night for classes overflowing from a nearby engineering school. If the reader happens to know all this—and that's not necessary, as we shall see—then he gets *the literal point* that Zukofsky and Miller taught poetry in the very building in which our greatest poet once worked. This is highly *ironic* because the building also becomes a place where engineering students can *resist poetry*. *But whether the reader gets this literal meaning is not so important perhaps as the symbolic sense*: The eagle is the national bird, and the fluted dome is, in Jefferson's standard architecture, another symbol of America.

The author relies on strong *metaphor*, especially at the beginning and end of the poem. These engineering students, in their suspicions that poetry is some kind of hoax, sit solid in their resistance to it the way a dam sits squarely in the path of a river. The metaphor is both apt and *ironic* because dams are built by engineers. Again, at the end, the metaphor involved is scientific. Anyone familiar with geometry knows if he finds out the length of the radius, he can figure out the length of the circumference. In both his personal advice and his poetry, Zukofsky *sounded only the radius,* letting his audience complete the picture for themselves.

The physical description of "Z" is accomplished in a series of *unexpected comparisons,* each one a separate *shock* intended to create an unforgettable image of the man. A grotesque caricature is risked here too—"Z"'s brows are so large he stands *in* them! Yet he is so slight, weightless, and tentative that he is likened to a *fly,* a creature that only *children* would be *candid* enough to compare with "Z".

Four times the author relies on puns. *Lou and I* takes on a special meaning as a repetition of *You and I.* And *Horace* suddenly becomes one of the *horrors.* Zukofsky has sent poems to *Botteghe Oscure,* a famous literary magazine whose title means, literally, *dark, dim, or obscure shops.* Miller comments that the magazine he publishes in is even *obscurer,* so much so that his poem is *catafalqued* (an unusual word meaning *laid out in a coffin*). In short, by being published in an obscure magazine, his poem has been killed. Another pun makes still another bitter point about the fate of the poet, alienated not only from his own classes but from the public at large. In ancient times, the rose was regarded as a symbol of privacy, secrecy, or silence. Today's poet, then, is not only working *under the rose* (usually we use the Latin *sub rosa*), he works under a *sootlined rose.* Again, *irony.* It's the engineers who produce the soot.

Like the man who *got RSVPs,* the author of "Z" counts on free associations, both his own and those of his readers. It is because he's loafing *à la* Whitman that the poet thinks of the *Eagle* building and hence associates to Lou. Scenes from their times together come to mind at random. And the final association is left to the reader to make. The young poet fails the older poet by refusing to accept praise. If he can't take praise, how does he receive love?

The final irony: The connection between these last two talks with "Z"—one about the young poet's work, the other about his marriage—occurs to the younger man only after "Z"'s death. It took the author of "Z: In Memory" a long, long time to complete the *total, terrorful circumference.*

Evaluating Poetry

We have shown you a reliable way to analyze and appreciate poetry. We can sum it up with a series of questions you can ask when you try to evaluate a poem.

☆ What *mood* does the poem create in you? Trust your own reactions! But get the mood before you get the meaning.

☆ How much of the *mood* is established by the poet's *music*? by his *stress* patterns? by his *tonal* patterns? Does he use *fixed meters, loose metrics,* or *free verse*? Does he set up tensions by creating a *rhythm* that resists the meter? How does this affect *message* as well as mood? What kinds of *matching sounds* does he use—full rhyme, assonance, dissonance (consonance), alliteration (initial rhyme)? How do his sounds — including *onomatopoeia*—contribute to mood? to *meaning*?

☆ Does he use (irregular) *strophes* or (regular) *stanzas*? How does his verse paragraph help unfold his message?

☆ What is the effect of the poet's use of *metaphor*? of *symbol*? *irony*? *paradox*? *allusion*? How effective is his *diction* when he makes *literal* statements?

☆ How much *specialized knowledge* is necessary for full appreciation of the poem?

☆ To what extent does the poem depend on the reader's ability to understand *free association*?

☆ Do any *phrases, images,* or *metaphors* remain in your memory? Why?

☆ How do *mood, music,* and *metaphor* blend into *meaning*?

☆ Has the poet stirred your imagination, roused your intellect, or struck a chord with your emotions? Has the poet's work given you new insights into human nature and the human condition?

Chapter 5

How to Analyze and Evaluate Nonfiction

The Cycle of Nonfiction

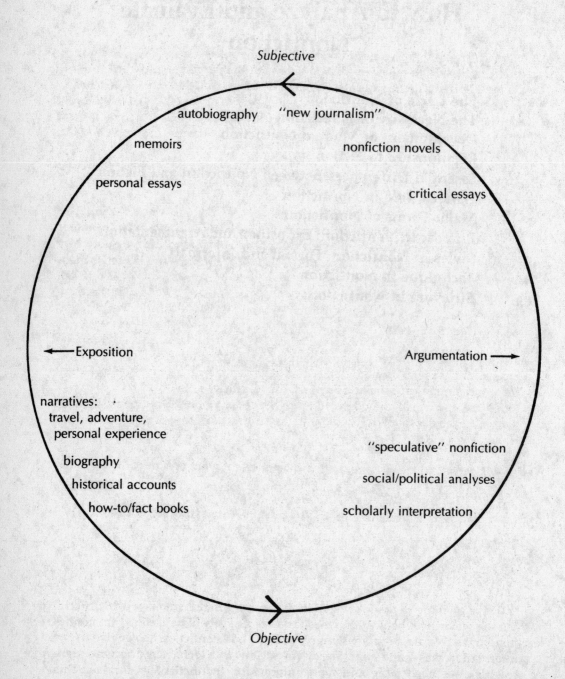

Subjective

autobiography   "new journalism"

memoirs   nonfiction novels

personal essays   critical essays

← Exposition   Argumentation →

narratives:
  travel, adventure,
  personal experience

  biography   "speculative" nonfiction

  historical accounts   social/political analyses

  how-to/fact books   scholarly interpretation

Objective

HOW TO ANALYZE AND
EVALUATE NONFICTION

Before you ran off to class this morning, you poured yourself a second cup of coffee and read the newspaper. You skimmed the headlines and zeroed in on the articles that caught your eye. One article discussed the events which led to the passage of a new tax law. Another was a profile of a rookie baseball player, another an angry editorial about education funding cutbacks, another a review of a jazz concert series, and yet another on energy-saving measures for the homeowner.

When you got to your first class and found that your next assignment was to write a report on a nonfiction book, you groaned. "Nonfiction? I wouldn't know *how* to write a report on nonfiction!"

Wrong! Think back to the morning paper. *The tax law article*: When you finished it, you finally understood why the new law was needed. *The rookie profile*: You noticed it downplayed his college record and didn't quote him directly. *The editorial*: You disagreed with some of the facts and statistics mentioned. *The jazz review*: You were intrigued, thought of buying tickets, although you thought the reviewer was pretty tough on one of the groups making a comeback. *The energy tips*: You felt some were too time-consuming, but that the tips on weatherstripping windows would be easy to follow.

The articles you read—and automatically criticized—were a sampling of the major nonfiction forms in miniature: mini-biography (profile), historical/process analysis (tax law article), criticism (jazz review), argumentation (editorial), and simple expository analysis (how-to article).

So, yes, you *would* know how to write a report on a nonfiction book, because your automatic responses focus on the key elements of reporting on nonfiction works:

★ *Content:*   Does it give me the information I want and need?

★ *Structure:*   Is it easy to follow and logical?

★ *Style:*   Is it presented in an imaginative, interesting fashion?

The Necessity of Nonfiction

We've all come to think of "literature" as being synonymous with "fiction." But the majority of books published (and the majority of bestsellers) are nonfiction books. We are a society hungry for facts, and nonfiction books give us the information we want—and need. As society and technology become more complex, we need more and more information (nonfiction) to survive. This explains, in part, the current boom in nonfiction on everything from how to buy a personal computer to how we got involved in Vietnam.

117

Development of Modern Nonfiction

But there is another reason behind the current popularity of nonfiction. In content, structure, and style, nonfiction has come of age as a legitimate literary genre.

Because people have always needed to communicate, nonfiction has always existed. But until this century, it was generally dry and didactic: travel documentaries, inspirational biographies, instructional texts, and the like.

The transformation began around the turn of the century when newspapers capitalized on the new "information technology"—telephones and telegraphs. People began to read more, and publishers began to compete for those readers. Reporters sent back dramatic on-the-scene accounts of battles, journalists gave in-depth reports on Wall Street and Washington, and "muckrakers" exposed corruption and exploitation. Upton Sinclair investigated the Chicago meat-packing industry as a journalist; Ernest Hemingway covered the Spanish Civil War as a journalist—and both are now remembered for writing classic works of fiction.

Relationship to Fiction

This crossover characterizes the second stage in the transformation of nonfiction. Fiction writers began using the tools of the journalist, and nonfiction writers began using the techniques of the novelist. This "new journalism" spawned a breed of nonfiction writers as artistic and expressive as any fiction writer, past or present. The traditional journalistic forms still dominate the front page of the newspaper, but the new journalism has left its mark everywhere else, from feature articles to full-length books.

The new nonfiction, using the techniques of fiction and drama, tends to be highly subjective. Dialogue and description, writer-as-participant, psychological insights, figurative language — all are now commonplace in nonfiction works. Anyone who has read Norman Mailer's *Armies of the Night*, an account of a march on the Pentagon in the 1960s, or Truman Capote's *In Cold Blood*, an analysis of a murder and execution, will understand why they are called "nonfiction novels." Nonfiction is based on fact. This essential difference between modern nonfiction and fiction is now the only difference. It is no longer valid to say one is more "creative" than the other.

Essential Differences Between Nonfiction and Fiction

While you'll use the same high standards in criticizing nonfiction as you would fiction, there are certain things about that essential difference you'll need to keep in mind.

A nonfiction writer *informs* you with the facts. But, by consciously selecting those facts, the writer can *persuade* you how to respond to those facts. You wouldn't question the "truth" or "accuracy" of fiction, but you must when you read nonfiction. Most important, you must think about what facts are *not* given. Highly personal works (autobiography, memoirs) use facts to "rationalize" behavior. Highly speculative works (future science, certain kinds of historical/social science analysis) use facts to "explain" the unknown. Highly opinionated works (criticism and interpretive analysis) use facts to "prove" a position. When you read such works, you must constantly decide whether you are being given a fair and accurate picture.

Another factor to keep in mind is the author's credentials. A fiction writer needn't be a spy to write a mystery. But a nonfiction writer had better be an expert to write about the history of orchid-raising in South America. And being an expert in one field doesn't qualify a writer to be an automatic expert in *any* field. The world's leading opera star might not be able to write a good book on international banking laws. So, just as you must check the completeness and accuracy of the information in a nonfiction work, you must check the author's qualifications for writing it.

Writer's Role in Nonfiction

By giving you some background on nonfiction, we hope to make your book report writing easier. There are other "behind-the-scenes" facts about nonfiction you should know too. Because contemporary nonfiction frequently uses fiction and drama techniques, the author is often visible throughout the work, whether as narrator or as participant. But you'll find many nonfiction works in which there is plenty of evidence of scholarship, yet no sign of the scholar.

This distinction between "subjectivity" and "objectivity" in nonfiction is similar to the range of points of view in fiction. So, just as different points of view create certain effects in a novel, you should examine the effects an author's choice of subjectivity or objectivity has on a nonfiction work.

This choice determines how *you* receive the information. Just as important, it determines the tone of the work. It is the key to the author's way of seeing and interpreting information.

Major Forms of Nonfiction

Nonfiction comes in many forms. Like poetry, it uses the form appropriate to the subject matter. By giving you a diagram showing the cycle of nonfiction and a breakdown of the major forms, their unique characteristics, and contemporary examples, we hope to make your nonfiction book report writing easier. While you read this section, remember that your book report itself will be a work of nonfiction. All of the structural devices and stylistic techniques we point out here are exactly what you can use in your own report writing.

Subjectivity: Autobiography and Memoirs

Autobiography and *memoirs* are personal narratives filled with anecdotes, character sketches, and opinions. Because they are highly subjective, you should evaluate them with the proverbial "grain of salt."

An autobiography usually focuses on a particular aspect of the author/subject's life — career, family relationships, spiritual/social awakening — to the necessary downplaying of other aspects. Its fictional counterpart would be the first-person narrative. Questions you would ask about such a fictional narrator's reliability and character will help you, too, when you evaluate an autobiography.

Politicians, celebrities, and popular "heroes" frequently write autobiographies. Usually they are honest, revealing glimpses of the private side of a public figure—but often, too, they are more glamor and gossip than anything else. So, you should always try to discover exactly what purpose the author had in writing his or her life story.

The following is a list of popular and contemporary autobiographies:

> *The Autobiography of Lincoln Steffens*
> *The Autobiography of Malcolm X*
> *Somebody Up There Likes Me* (Rocky Graziano)
> *Lauren Bacall By Myself*

Memoirs, too, are first-person narratives, but of a broader scope and purpose than autobiography. Memoirs are the author/narrator's "memory" of a particular time or event and the people involved. Eileen Simpson's *Poets in Their Youth* is a sensitive recollection of American poets she knew, such as John Berryman and Robert Lowell. *Ease My Sorrows*, by Lev Kopelev, is the harrowing and philosophical reminiscence of his years in a Soviet gulag along with Solzhenitsyn.

You will find that setting and characterization are crucial to the memoir, as the author is recreating the personalities and flavor of the past. The memoir's author is not the subject, as is the autobiography's author, but it is important that you establish the author's relationship to the events and people discussed. Again, you must ask yourself what the author's purpose was in writing the memoir: to shed new light, offer a new perspective on an important event? to point the finger at someone's guilt or responsibility for a scandal or tragedy? to give a bystander's account, a minor eyewitness' version of a momentous historical event? Whatever the case, you'll need to be aware of the central fact that this is history through the eyes and ears of one person.

Some notable and controversial memoirs include *Bring Me A Unicorn*, by Anne Morrow Lindbergh, wife of the aviator Charles Lindbergh; *Don't Fall Off the Mountain*, by actress Shirley MacLaine; and Henry Kissinger's memoirs of his years in the Nixon administration, *White House Years*.

Objectivity: Biography and Historical Narrative

You'll notice that autobiography and memoir are on the *subjective* side of the nonfiction cycle. The *objective* counterpart of a person's life story is the *biography*.

Written in the third person, biographies are usually the carefully researched and documented works of a journalist/scholar. They can range from the reconstruction of a historical personality in ancient Greece to a heady, fan-club portrait of a rock star or soap opera heroine. (Many "biographies" of celebrities are unauthorized by the celebrity. That is, he or she neither gave permission for it to be written nor had any control over the final contents. Be wary of these gossipy, distorted books.)

The true aim of biography is to give a balanced picture of a personality unfolding. You'll find that characterization is the main concern of a good biography, and that the events and focus which shaped the personality will be examined in detail. These psychological insights are the "clues" a good biographer follows. So, in some respects, a well-written biography is like a well-plotted mystery.

Biographies always have been and continue to be popular. Here are a few classic examples:

> *Lou Gehrig: A Quiet Hero*, Frank L. Graham
> *The Life, Legends, and Madness of Howard Hughes*, Donald L.
>   Bartlett and James B. Steele
> *Callas*, John Ardoin and Gerald Fitzgerald
> *Microbe Hunters*, Paul De Kruif

The objective counterpart of the memoir is the *historical narrative*. Like biography, the historical narrative is based on solid research and a reasoned interpretation of the facts; like memoirs, it focuses on the central figures and events of a particular period.

You read historical narrative every time you read the newspaper: background information about the social conditions of working class British teenagers explains where punk rock comes from; background information on the Islamic rejection of western ideals explains why the Shah of Iran was overthrown.

Often you'll read historical narrative on distant events that reads as dramatically as any work of fiction. By reconstructing "dialogue" on the basis of diaries, letters, and eyewitness accounts, writers of historical narratives can weave fragments of the past into realistic, immediate adventure. You would never think of the Battle of Gettysburg as some vague date in history after reading the tragic, human reconstruction of Michael Saara's *The Killer Angels*.

The New Science: Speculative Nonfiction

One of the major forms of modern nonfiction is what we call *speculative nonfiction*. Just as science fiction takes natural laws one step beyond, speculative nonfiction projects into the future—or the prehistoric past—using scientific theories and methods, and proven historical facts. Every time you read about the origin of the universe, the possibility of extrasensory perception, the role of artificial intelligence and robots in future society, you are reading speculative nonfiction.

It is one of the most exciting developments in contemporary nonfiction. For the first time, theoretical scientists and social scientists are writing elegant works about unknown worlds for popular audiences. Fritjof Capra's *The Tao of Physics* explores the relationship between quantum physics and ancient Eastern philosophy. The many works of Carl Sagan discuss extraterrestrial life and interplanetary travel. Elisabeth Kübler-Ross's work with terminally ill patients led her to recount their fascinating near-death—or after-death—experiences.

But a word of caution: The credentials of the speculative nonfiction writer are crucial. No reputable scientist, such as those we've just mentioned, would risk his or her professional reputation with shoddy research or a half-baked hypothesis. But there are nonscientific "authorities" who try to cash in on the current popularity of speculative nonfiction with sensational books about UFOs, mysterious gods from outer space, and ghostly visits from great-aunt Agatha. You can spot these shoddy works quickly: They are hysterical in tone and lack any conclusive evidence for the "theories" they claim to prove.

Collections and Anthologies: Nonfiction Samplers

The final major category of nonfiction books is the *collection* or *anthology*. A long-respected format for short stories and poetry, the *collection/anthology* is fast becoming a popular format for every form and style of nonfiction writing.

A *collection* is a book-length set of short works by a single author; an *anthology* contains the works of several authors. Most creative writers, no matter what their literary specialty, publish short nonfiction pieces in magazines or newspapers: essays, reviews, interviews, feature articles. The author (or an editor) selects the best work for a collection. *Picked-Up Pieces*, John Updike's book reviews; *Wallflower at the Orgy*, Nora Ephron's humorous views on current events and popular tastes; and the dramatic sketches in Truman Capote's *Music for Chameleons* are excellent examples.

One of the things you should look for in a collection is the purpose. Why were *these* particular pieces selected? Perhaps they are all about the same subject— modern art, for instance. Or perhaps they give you a sampling of the writer's styles, techniques, and moods. Or perhaps they show the growth and development of the writer's skill and philosophy. A collection shouldn't strike you as being a hodgepodge or a repetitious bore.

The purpose of an *anthology* must be clearly evident, because several "voices" are speaking. An anthology often showcases the works of a particular social group—Amerindians, blue-collar workers, religious leaders. If so, you should be able to see a "profile" of the group's beliefs and concerns, and perspectives emerge from the anthology. Another variety focuses on a particular topic— nuclear weapons, for instance—and may give you a cross-section of viewpoints. In either case, you should consider whether the "voices" chosen are representative of the group and whether the viewpoints are balanced and fair. And, again, you should consider the merits of the individual pieces, both as self-contained units and as parts of the whole.

Purpose in Nonfiction: Exposition and Argumentation

As we move onto the second half of the nonfiction cycle, we want to give you some perspective on the material we've just covered and an overview of what comes next.

If you look at the diagram at the beginning of this chapter again, you'll see that we've been discussing the "poles" of subjectivity and objectivity in nonfiction, and one-half of the forms divided by those poles. That portion consists of *expository* nonfiction: factual, informative, explanatory. The next portion of the cycle consists of *argumentative* nonfiction: critical, interpretive, reasoned.

As we mentioned earlier in the chapter, writers can use facts to inform you or to persuade you. This, then, is the basic difference between *exposition* and *argumentation*. You may find it difficult to see the difference at first, especially when the work is highly subjective. But a simple question will help you: Are the facts presented in such a way that I'm free to reach my own conclusions about their significance?

If your answer is "yes," then you are reading expository nonfiction. If your answer is "no," then you are reading argumentative nonfiction. You read both kinds of nonfiction every day. A news article about teenage unemployment rates just gives the facts. But an editorial on teenage unemployment rates, using those same facts, builds a case to support an opinion on the subject. In the first case, you're free to draw any conclusion about the facts; in the second, you are led step-by-step to see the writer's conclusions.

Styles of Nonfiction: Formal and Informal

Nonfiction books are based on the stylistic and technical principles of the *essay*. By giving you brief explanations of those styles and techniques, we'll be giving you a twofold bonus: First, you'll be better able to analyze how a nonfiction book is constructed; second, you'll be able to write a better book report. Remember, your report is itself a critical essay.

Essays and books—particularly argumentative essays and books—are written in either *formal style* or *informal style*. The distinction between the two styles is similar to the distinction between subjective and objective nonfiction. But the central difference is the structural approach used to "build a case," how the major conclusion is presented.

Formal style is serious, carefully balanced, and rather impersonal. You can detect immediately what the writer's position is on the subject, because it's usually stated clearly after a brief introduction, whether just a paragraph (in an essay), or a brief first chapter (in a book).

The "body"—the middle section—of formal argumentative nonfiction is a series of logical, step-by-step mini-conclusions supported by pertinent facts and examples. All of this leads to an acceptable conclusion as neatly as a geometric proof.

The classic example of formal style would be any of the essays of Francis Bacon. A perfectly good contemporary example would be a thoughtful editorial in any newspaper. Next time you read one, see if you can outline it. You'll find it almost always follows this format. Book-length works of this style are based on the same format, only more fully developed and comprehensive. Any work advocating a particular viewpoint on a controversial subject—politics, science, culture—is written in this way.

Informal style is harder to pin down. It is highly personal, impressionistic, dramatic, and the structure is more psychological than logical. If you go looking for a clearly stated position, you *may* find it towards the end. But more often it is implied rather than stated in the overall tone, the choice of examples, the stylistic techniques.

Here your familiarity with the newspaper helps out. The feature article about teenage unemployment—the human interest story—will differ greatly from the straight news story or the editorial. The informal feature article *shows* you the writer's position; the news story and the editorial *tell* you. Books on the human condition and human behavior, such as *Black Like Me* by Michael Harrington, a white man's disguised journey as a black man in the South, or Joan Didion's *The White Album*, a numbing kaleidoscope of observations of the tumultous Sixties, are frequently written in informal style. Humorous and philosophical books, too, are popular in this style.

Technique in Nonfiction

But whether the author chooses to state or imply the book's central point, he or she uses the same techniques to support it. And, by learning to identify these techniques, you'll be better equipped to analyze the book—and to use those same techniques in your book report.

Narration is, simply, telling a story. When you summarize a plot or give background information to support a point you're making, you're narrating.

Description is providing physical or sensory detail so that the reader—your report reader—"sees" the same thing you do. You do this when you describe a stranger's face to your friend or when you give the specific details of setting in a short story.

Definition is explaining the meaning of a word or an abstract concept. A strange object in a science fiction novel needs to be defined, as would the meaning of "surrealism." People very often disagree on the exact meaning of abstract concepts—like freedom or honor—so it's very important that you explain how *you* mean to use the term by defining it early in your report.

Examples and *anecdotes* are specific instances of a point or fact. Examples are brief details; anecdotes are dramatizations of those details. For instance, to show that a particular character in a novel was generous, you can give an example: He donated $500 to charity every New Year's Day. Or, you could provide an anecdote that *showed* him being generous, perhaps a scene described by his daughter about the time he bought lunch for a busload of students stranded at an airport.

A writer uses all of these techniques to support a point or build up to a conclusion, whether the work is written in formal or informal style. Any work claiming to present a position or prove a point which doesn't provide these particulars is fatally flawed. Be on the lookout for works filled with generalizations, scare-tactic warnings, or lopsided "evidence." A solid opinion is supported by facts—if it's not, then it's just a prejudice.

Structure in Nonfiction

We've given you the major styles and approaches you'll find in argumentative nonfiction books. Although they'll differ as widely as the investigative analysis

The Case Against Congress by Jack Anderson and Drew Pearson and the philosophical musings of *Pilgrim at Tinker Creek* by Annie Dillard, they will share a basic structural characteristic: any part is a reflection of the whole.

Both novels and nonfiction books are broken into chapters. But, while novel chapters can vary greatly in many respects, nonfiction chapters should be consistent miniatures of the structure, style, and content of the complete book.

Think of an argumentative nonfiction book as a chain, with each chapter a link. Solid argumentation is a carefully forged chain of evidence, reasons, and conclusions. If a link is weak or missing, the whole chain falls apart.

Evaluating Nonfiction

Now that you are familiar with the styles, techniques, and forms available to nonfiction writers, you can judge your assigned book with confidence.

☆ Which major *form of nonfiction* best describes the book? Does the book provide the *content, structure,* and *style* needed to fulfill that form's *purpose*?

☆ What role does the book's author play? Does this *point of view* relate to the *theme* and *tone*?

☆ What *fictional or dramatic techniques* does the author use? How do they contribute to the book's *purpose*?

☆ How important is *setting* or *characterization*? Does the book's author handle them imaginatively?

☆ How would you describe *the author's characteristic use of language*? Does he or she use *figures of speech*? How would you describe the *diction*? the *sentence maneuvers*? the pacing of words and phrases to build *suspense*? How does all of this relate to the book's *theme* and the form's *purpose*?

☆ How reliable and thorough is the author? Is the material in the book presented fairly and completely? or is the book biased? Does the author seem qualified to write the book?

☆ Was the book written to *inform* (*expository* nonfiction) or to *persuade* (*argumentative* nonfiction)? If written to persuade, how successfully does the author present *evidence* for the book's *conclusions*?

☆ Is the book written in *formal style* or *informal style*? How does this affect the book's *tone*? How well does this fit with the book's *purpose* and *conclusions*?

☆ How well do the individual parts of the book fit within the entire book? What special function does each part play in the book's overall *purpose* and *theme*?

Chapter 6

Reading and Writing Critically

The Key to Writing Book Reports
Learning to Read Critically
Using Your Chapter Checklists
Planning Your Book Report
Sharpening Your Focus
Analyzing Your Topic
Supporting Your Topic
Refining Your Topic
Introductions and Conclusions

READING AND WRITING CRITICALLY

The Key to Writing Book Reports

As paradoxical as it sounds, the best way to analyze a book or play is to "read it backwards." All this really means is that it's impossible for you to understand the significance of the beginning until you've reached the end.

When you finish reading a well-plotted mystery, your first reaction might be, "Of course! I should have known all along! The clues were right there all the time!" Although not quite so dramatic, your reaction to any creative work will be similar. The conclusion, the overall impression, will strike you as effortless and inevitable. The key to writing a superior book report, then, is the ability to go back and find the "clues," the specific examples, that help you explain *your* conclusions and overall impressions.

For example, after reading one of Edgar Allan Poe's short stories, you might feel the tone is overwhelmingly oppressive and sinister. After thinking about this impression, you might suggest it is the setting, more so than the plot or characters, that is chiefly responsible for this chilling effect.

Now, like the detective, you go back to specific passages of description to confirm, or disprove, your hunch. And there, yes, you find vivid details of rotted crossbeams, darkened corners, moonless skies, foggy moors. You would then examine other passages to see if they, too, impart the same depressing mood.

Here, then, you have the essential elements of your book report: *the subject* (one of Poe's short stories); *the topic* (the sinister tone of that short story); *the focus* (how the setting creates the sinister tone).

Learning to Read Critically

Although you *can* go back and reread the entire work before you write your report, it isn't always possible. What is essential is that you *read critically the first time*. Whether you're reporting on a poem, a short story, a novel, a play, or a nonfiction book, you must begin your task well-equipped. And you do this by understanding the characteristics of a particular genre and by familiarizing yourself with key literary concepts.

Using Your Chapter Checklists

In previous chapters, we covered each of the genres at length and have provided you with selected literary concepts. To plunge into writing your book report without having read these chapters carefully would be like visiting a foreign country without a map or phrase book. You would quickly become confused and frustrated. So, once you've studied the "map" and "phrases," you're ready to read the work confidently.

To help you on your literary journey, at the end of this book we've provided a Book Report Worksheet and a Chapter Checklist. Although you may not need to fill in every section, we urge you to pause and absorb what you've read in each chapter (or section or act), then answer as many of the questions as possible.

The questions are specific and will require careful writing. But they have a twofold benefit.

★ First, because they zero in on specifics, they alert you to the building blocks of the entire work. Thus, in addition to helping you analyze small portions of a complete work, they clue you in as to what to look for in succeeding chapters.

★ Second, they provide a tremendous outline of the entire work when you've finished reading. So, instead of spending hours flipping pages in search of a crucial example, a turning point, a shift in point of view, you'll be able to study your chapter checklists. They become the map from which you'll plot your route—your report.

You can, of course, supplement this approach by highlighting passages or by making notes in the margins (as long as you own the book!) or by jotting down page references and comments on the back of your chapter checklist.

Planning Your Book Report

Now you're ready to plan your book report. Just as you must read the work critically, you must plan the report carefully. And, unless you plan on writing a ten-volume analysis covering *every* aspect and feature of the work, you need to zero in on your topic, decide on your focus, and choose your approach and emphasis.

Think back to the example of Poe's short story. The topic was the tone, and the focus — the basic structure of your report — would be cause and effect analysis, how the setting "causes" the tone.

Of course, not all book reports are based on that same outline. But it does show you how to plan writing a book report. *"What is the relationship between X and Y?"* is the central question to ask after you've reviewed your chapter checklists. What is the relationship between the methods of characterization and the theme? Between the subplot and the main plot? Between the point of view and the imagery? Very often this question sparks an imaginative, exciting book report—far more interesting to write (and to read!) than the dull summary ending with "and I would recommend it to all my friends."

Sharpening Your Focus

As a further aid, in Chapter 8 we've provided "Questions to Ask" that will help you sharpen your focus and refine your approach. An excellent review of major elements in creative work, the "Questions to Ask" section, beginning on page 146, contains specific questions you can choose as the focus for your own book report. And a reminder: Whatever focus/approach you decide on should match the complexity of your subject. Don't overanalyze a short poem—and don't skim through the analysis of a long novel!

Analyzing Your Topic

There are, of course, many structures you can use when writing a book report, depending on the focus you choose. But the essential structure—the bedrock of *all* writing—is simple analysis, breaking down a topic into its basic parts or stages.

Let's say the topic you choose is the rise and fall of a particular character's fortunes. It will be a lot easier to write about that rise and fall if you discuss individual stages in the series of stages, rather than try to tackle the rise and fall as one sweeping whole. Or, let's say the topic you choose is a writer's imagery. You could break that down into types or categories of imagery: imagery used when describing setting, when describing action, etc.

The key, of course, in a good simple analysis is deciding on "pieces" that are parallel and equal in importance. You wouldn't want to strain your reader's belief by comparing apples and radiators, or by using vague or irrelevant examples. A good simple analysis is built of compatible parts and significant examples.

Supporting Your Topic

Whether your book report will be on a work of fiction, poetry, drama, or nonfiction, it's important that you read the chapter on nonfiction thoroughly before you write your report. Your book report is, after all, a work of nonfiction!

It would also be helpful to remember that, since your report is essentially an argumentative essay, you need to support your conclusions and impressions with specific examples from the assigned work. Using the outline you construct after reviewing your chapter checklists, you can then go back to select quotable passages that best illustrate the "pieces" in your outline. There's no magic number, actually, but it's a good idea to have three examples for every major point you make.

Let's return to the topic of a writer's imagery. You decide to examine the language used when the writer is describing (1) people, (2) setting, and (3) action. You then refer to your chapter checklist for clues. Where is a new character, setting, or action described? You examine those passages, and then select three of the best examples for each. The most orderly—and time-saving—method is to copy each quote exactly (*verbatim*) on a separate index card, noting the page number.

Refining Your Topic

This is the stage in your writing when a very curious thing often happens. While studying and reviewing *just* the writer's imagery, you might notice, say, that the writer tends to use similes, rather than metaphors. But you might also see, now that the passages are standing alone, that there are *patterns* in the words the writer uses. You might suddenly realize that all descriptions of people contain words associated with animals ("snorted," "barked," "She had the eyes of a cornered rabbit"); or that all descriptions of action contain words associated with machinery ("arms pumping like pistons," "the argument picked up steam").

Discovering the patterns in a work is the ultimate goal of your book report. Once you have found them, you can sharpen the focus of the report and thereby streamline the entire writing process. Whereas you started out with only a fragmented thought for each part of your rough outline ("*imagery used when describing people*"), you now have a highly polished, complete *statement*, supported by specific examples. "*In John Smith's novel, descriptions of people frequently contain animal imagery.*"

And there you have an excellent basis for refining your outline—indeed, the entire report—even further. You might focus on this "piece" as the beginning of a new outline, breaking it down into new "pieces"—descriptions of men, of women, of elderly people, etc. In turn, all of these polished statements—miniconclusions, so to speak—show you exactly how to go back and refine, polish, focus your report's main topic until it glows.

So, as paradoxical as it seemed to hear that the best way to analyze a work is to read it backwards, you can now relax when we say that the best way to write a book report is "backwards," too! It involves a continual process of refining your original topic.

Introductions and Conclusions

All of what we've just described centers on the *body* of your book report. The beginning and the end—the introduction and the final conclusion—are written *after* you have developed and refined the body. (How else do you know what you're introducing?)

The introductory section of your book report is composed of the *identification* and *definition* of the work, and its *context*. Simply, the identification includes the work's title (and source, if part of a large work) and author. The definition is the work's genre and type: *gothic horror* novel, *surrealistic* poem, *classical* tragedy.

Normally, though, you need to include more information about the work if you want the reader to understand its importance. This should include significant facts about the work's context, facts that locate the work in time or tradition.

All of this introductory information is then shaped to lead smoothly and logically to the polished, focused statement of your report's topic.

In the final section—the critical conclusion—you give your judgment of the work's success. You can consider many factors when making this decision. Did it keep your interest? Was the author's chosen form and structure appropriate to the theme? Was the theme believable and well supported? (See Chapter 1 for a complete discussion of approaches and emphases for your conclusion.)

If, after you examine your notes, checklists, and impressions, you're not enthusiastic about the work, it's important that you explain why. To shrug a work off as "boring" or "unbelievable" is to cancel out all the effort you put into reading and analyzing it. Be precise: Say, "it was boring *because* . . . ," "it was unbelievable *because* . . . ." As a critical reader, you're well-equipped and qualified to state a conclusion based on your observations and impressions.

Keep in mind that your final assessment of the work is not an artificial, tagged-on ending. Everything you wrote before it actually leads up to your conclusion. In other words, the position you take and the supporting examples and explanations you give in the body of your book report should lead you—and the reader of your report—to your critical conclusion.

Chapter 7

How to Use Quotations and Footnotes

Selecting Quotable Material
Documenting Your Quotations Properly

HOW TO USE QUOTATIONS AND FOOTNOTES

Many students dread writing book reports, not because they dislike reading or analyzing a book, but because they dislike the formal methods of preparation required. But this dread is unnecessary, as the methods are quite simple and logical. The following guidelines should make your book report writing much easier, especially if you keep them in mind while you are reading the assigned book.

Selecting Quotable Material

The most common mistake students make when writing a book report is thinking that the report must be crammed with quotes. Not only does this create tremendous work for you, but it also results in a boring, stilted report. The purpose of the report is to demonstrate your critical understanding—not your typing gymnastics!

As you read the assigned book, your ability to spot significant passages and typical examples of an author's style will develop rapidly if you follow the suggestions we made in previous chapters. Your chapter-by-chapter summaries (or your scene-by-scene summaries) will help you zero in on passages suitable for quoting.

Not only that, but as you refine your approach and begin to decide how best to judge the work, you will automatically spot significant passages as you read them, and can thus make note of them. The art of book report writing comes with careful selection of as few examples from the assigned work as are needed to make your point clear. You do *not* need to stuff each paragraph with wholesale passages and long, tedious quotes.

Once you have selected the passages you want to use as direct quotes, you need to understand three points: (1) how to avoid quoting out of context; (2) how to deal with long quotes; and (3) how to document the quotation properly.

Keep Your Quotes in Context

Quoting material out of context is actually a twofold problem. Inexperienced writers sometimes quote half of a sentence from the original text, thereby distorting the meaning. Or, they use the complete passage about Topic A, but they use it in a section on Topic B, thereby presenting inaccurate evidence in support of Topic B.

Both of these errors can be avoided if you follow two simple rules:

1. Always make sure that the quoted material means *exactly* the same thing to your reader as it did when you read it in the assigned book.

2. Always introduce a quotation with a sentence explaining its importance and relationship to the point you are making.

A simple introductory statement (such as: *The protagonist's anger is clear throughout the first chapter. For example, ". . . ."*) serves the dual purpose of presenting the point you are making (*the protagonist is angry*) and of providing a smooth transition for the quote. To plop a quote on a page without such an introductory statement is to confuse the reader and muddy your point.

Three Methods of Using Long Quotations

Very often a long passage in a book best illustrates the point you want to make. But a long quotation is often clumsy and distracting. In this case you have three methods to choose from:

1. paraphrase the long quotation

2. edit (emend) the long quotation

3. use the entire long quotation, employing the specific forms required

To *paraphrase* means to boil down the meaning, the gist, of a long passage into your own words. It is an *indirect* method of quoting. But even though *you* rephrased the passage, the ideas are *not* yours—*they must be documented with a footnote at the end of your paraphrase.* Beginning writers sometimes mistakenly think that a paraphrased passage does not need a footnote. This naive error can result in your being accused of *plagiarism.* So, as a rule of thumb, you must document anyone else's *ideas,* whether quoted directly or indirectly.

The second method of presenting a long quotation is to edit it. This means eliminating sections of the passage not absolutely essential to the point you're making while still preserving the direct quotation itself. To indicate where you left out material in the passage, simply insert an *ellipsis* (. . .) and continue with the quotation. If you are leaving out the end of a sentence in a long quotation, you indicate that by adding a period to the ellipsis (. . . .).

Frequently, this edited version of the quotation will have gaps in meaning because specific names or facts have been cut out. You need to restore these specifics accurately somewhere in the new edited version. For example, let's say that in the uncut original quotation a Mr. Jones is mentioned specifically once, and is referred to as "he" or "him" thereafter. In your edited version, you've cut out the part containing "Mr. Jones," leaving only an unidentified "he" or "him." What you must do is insert [Mr. Jones] instead of "he" the first time "he" appears in the edited version.

Bracketed material within a quotation is always recognized as the work of the writer/editor. So you will often see such forms as ". . . and so [the teachers] left the building," or "Mr. Cataldo [Brown's attorney] refused to comment on the subject." Both of these examples indicate the writer/editor's attempt to clarify edited quoted material.

There are other instances, too, when you should use the editorial bracket. If the quoted material contains an error, whether in spelling, grammar, or fact, you must indicate that the error exists *in the original text,* and is not a mistake *you* have made. This is done by adding [sic]. For example: "Harley complained about the poor service he recieved [sic] at the restaurant."

Another instance when the editorial bracket should be used is when you want to emphasize words or phrases in a quotation by using *italics.* As the italics did not exist in the original, you must indicate that *you* added them by inserting [author emphasis] or [author italics]. For example: "Chi swore he had never been to San Diego, yet *seventeen people identified him as the man at Mrs. Hong's funeral"* [author italics].

Should you decide to use the third method—to quote a lengthy passage in its entirety—you must be sure of several things: one, that you aren't resorting to wholesale quoting just to fill space or, two, just trying to save yourself the effort of rethinking, paraphrasing, and/or editing the material.

You can resist these temptations by remembering that an *extended quotation* should not exceed ten single-spaced typed lines. Once you have selected the passage (perhaps after paraphrasing a bit, editing a bit), there is an acceptable format you can follow.

As you know, a brief quotation is contained within the normal double-spaced text of your book report. It is set off by quotation marks with a *superscript number* indicating its footnote at the end of the quotation.

The extended quotation differs considerably. It is "blocked off" from the normal double-spaced text and has wider left and right margins than the text. It is *not* set off by quotation marks, and it is single-spaced. The superscript, however, remains the same.

If you are in doubt as to whether or not a quotable passage should be contained within the text or "blocked off," keep this rule in mind: Any quotation that would take up more than three normal double-spaced lines should be converted to a "blocked off" extended quotation.

Documenting Your Quotations Properly

Documenting your quotations in a book report is relatively easy. Unlike term papers, which require references from many different sources, a book report is based solely on one book. So your only decision would be *which* form of documentation to use. Three different forms may be used for fiction and nonfiction books—prose works—and you should check with your teacher as to which form is preferred. Drama and poetry have specific forms which we will discuss separately.

Internal Reference

The *internal reference* form requires only one footnote at the bottom of the first page of your book report. There you give a complete footnote reference and a brief statement that all further references will be to the same source. After that first reference to your assigned book, a parenthetical reference—an internal page reference—is placed after each new quotation or paraphrase. No further footnotes or superscript numbers are necessary. For example: ". . . to see you again" (p. 47).

Footnotes and Endnotes

Footnotes and *endnotes*, the other two forms, differ only in the placement of the reference. If you use footnotes, all quotations made on a given page are cited at the bottom, or foot, of that page. If you are using endnotes, all references are listed on a separate page at the *end* of the entire book report. In both cases, the superscript numbers run consecutively throughout the entire book report.

How Footnotes and Bibliographies Differ

Again, because a book report is based solely on one book, you will not need a bibliography. But it would make it easier for you to remember correct footnote/ endnote form if you understood the differences between a footnote entry and a bibliographic entry.

The purpose of a footnote is to tell the reader exactly where to find a particular passage in a particular book. So a footnote entry will always include a page reference. A bibliographic entry does not.

The focus of a footnote is on the title, the author, and the page reference. All other information about the book — place of publication, publisher, date of publication—is not as significant and so is couched in parentheses. There are no parentheses in a bibliographic entry.

The purpose and focus of a bibliographic entry is to help a curious reader find the book as easily as possible in a card catalogue in the library. The entry begins with the author's last name, which allows for easy indexing and alphabetization. Because this would be the first clue a curious reader would look for, the bibliographic entry begins with a five-space "overhang." The footnote entry, on the other hand, begins with a five-space indentation.

Here are examples of (1) a footnote entry and (2) a bibliographic entry for the same book:

[3]Joan Didion, *The White Album* (New York: Washington Square Press, 1979), p. 47.

Didion, Joan. *The White Album*. New York: Washington Square Press, 1979.

If the book is an anthology or collection put together by an editor, rather than written by a single author:

[7]Oscar Williams, ed., *Master Poems of the English Language* (New York: Washington Square Press, 1966), p. 127.

Williams, Oscar, ed. *Master Poems of the English Language*. New York: Washington Square Press, 1966.

If it is an original work which has been translated or edited:

[5]Umberto Eco, *The Name of the Rose*, trans. William Weaver (New York: Harcourt Brace Jovanovich, 1983), pp. 43-47.

Eco, Umberto. *The Name of the Rose*. Translated by William Weaver. New York: Harcourt Brace Jovanovich, 1983.

There are other variations, too, depending upon additional information about the assigned book. For these more complicated entries, you should refer to guidebooks written specifically for this purpose, such as:

Keyworth, Cynthia. *How to Write a Term Paper*. New York: Arco Publishing, Inc., 1982.

The only variation you need to know is the special streamlined footnote form to be used after the first complete reference to a book. It would be time-consuming to repeat the entire footnote over and over! After having read the first full footnote, your reader needs only to know the new page reference. So the second and subsequent references to your assigned book are written this way:

²Ibid., p. 27.

If the new reference is to the same page cited in the previous footnote, you need only to write:

³Ibid.

If you have paraphrased material which covered several pages in the original, you would indicate that in this way:

⁴Ibid., pp. 22–24.

This paraphrase reference form is used, too, in a complete footnote. Please note that Ibid. is *not* underlined/italicized.

These forms are acceptable for all books, fiction or nonfiction, with one exception. References to a passage in the Bible require only the name of the book, the chapter, and the verse, whether as an internal reference (Luke 2:24) or as a footnote/endnote. Again, the name of the book is not underlined/italicized.

²Luke 2:24

Proper References for Drama, Poetry, and Short Stories

Two different forms are used for identifying quotations from dramatic works. The first form, used for footnotes/endnotes, resembles the entry for books. The second form, used for internal references, resembles the entry for the Bible.

¹Shakespeare, *Macbeth*, act 2, sc. 1, lines 5–10.

(*Macbeth* II:i:5–10)

Note that the first form uses all Arabic numerals, and the second form uses Roman numerals for act and scene.

As poems are usually part of a larger work (as are articles in a magazine, chapters in a book), the title of a poem (or an article or chapter) is placed within quotation marks, as only the title of a book is underlined/italicized.

The first footnote/endnote reference to a poem includes complete information about the book in which it appears, along with specific verse and line references:

[1]William Blake, "The Tyger," *Master Poems of the English Language*, ed. Oscar Williams (New York: Washington Square Press, 1966), v.2, lines 3–4.

Short stories, too, are usually parts of a larger whole. References to a short story will be like those to a poem, except that a page reference will come at the end, rather than a verse and line reference:

[1]F. Scott Fitzgerald, "The Freshest Boy," *Taps at Reveille* (New York: Curtis Publishing Company, 1928), p. 36.

Chapter 8

Putting It All Together:
The Book Report

A Final Review: Questions to Ask
Further Thoughts on Style
Questions to Ask: Language and Structure
Questions to Ask: Characterization
Questions to Ask: Theme
Chapter Checklist
Book Report Worksheets

A Final Review: Questions to Ask

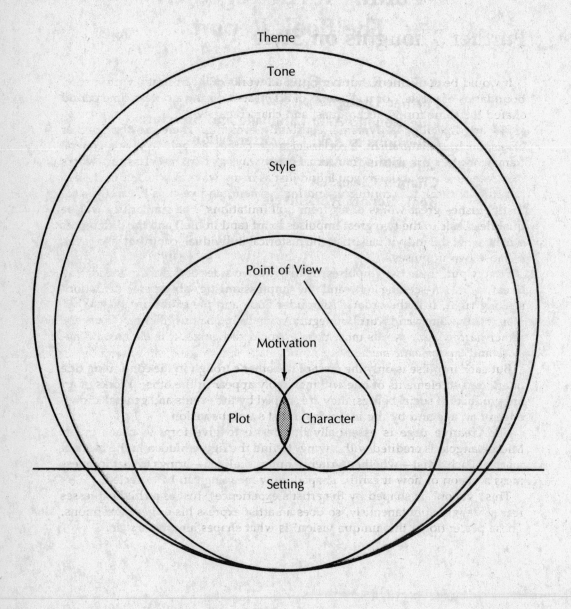

Theme

Tone

Style

Point of View

Motivation

Plot

Character

Setting

PUTTING IT ALL TOGETHER: THE BOOK REPORT

Further Thoughts on Style

It would be convenient, but boring, if all works of art fit neatly within strict boundaries of "style," or if all works of art created during a certain time period shared the same forms, techniques, and characteristics.

But art, like life, is dynamic, constantly evolving. There are the familiar labels, such as Naturalism, Neoclassicism, and they do help to give a general framework to work within, but for as many ways as two "neoclassical" works may resemble one another, you'll find just as many ways in which they differ.

You may think this confusing and inconsistent, and yet this is exactly what distinguishes great works of art from dull imitations. The similarities will be qualities basic to the two great impulses in art (and in life!) and the differences will be what the individual artist, the historical individual, contributes to either of those two impulses.

Simply put, these two impulses are like the two sides of the brain: the logical, linear, solution-seeking left, and the impressionistic, absorbent, sensation-seeking right. It is the orderly Alexander Pope and the exuberant Walt Whitman; Henry James and Kurt Vonnegut; Aristotle and Samuel Beckett. To use the rather narrow code words most people would recognize, it is *the classical impulse* and *the romantic impulse.*

But each impulse is only the crest of the other's trough in the continuing tide of art, and so elements of one will inevitably appear in the other. Works of art are products of social beings; they are shaped by the events and general knowledge of an age and by the individual artist's unique vision.

The creative urge is essentially the desire to give form to chaos or, as Michaelangelo is credited with saying, to find the figure hidden in the block of marble. Each artist—whether writer, painter, sculptor—brings to that formless mass a vision of how it can be shaped, how meaning can be extracted.

This "vision" is shaped by the artist's experiences. Just as a child expresses fear or delight spontaneously, so does an artist express his or her perceptions. These perceptions, this unique vision, is what shapes an artist's *style.*

Questions to Ask: Language and Structure

The *expression* of an idea (language) and the *form* of that expression (structure) should be appropriate to the *idea* (theme).

☆ Does the author tend to use *denotative* (factual) or *connotative* (suggestive, qualitative) words and phrases?

☆ Are descriptive passages *literal* (concrete, specific) or *figurative* (abstract, comparative)?

☆ Are the figures of speech (similes, metaphors, symbols) consistent with the tone and theme?

☆ Does the author's characteristic way of forming sentences relate in any way to the point of view? to the tone? to the theme?

☆ How would you describe the author's tone? Is it consistent throughout the work?

☆ Does the story follow strict chronology? or does the work begin *in medias res* and use flashbacks?

☆ What is the proportion of scenic to narrative passages? How is this significant overall?

Questions to Ask: Characterization

Major (main) characters are fully developed and undergo change; *minor* characters are merely revealed and remain static.

☆ What function do the individual minor characters play?

☆ What motivates the individual characters, especially the main, focus character?

☆ In what ways—and in what proportions—does the author reveal personality?

☆ What effect does setting have on the focus character?

☆ What effect does the narrator/point of view have on your understanding of the focus character?

☆ What kind of imagery is used to describe the focus character?

☆ Does the focus character act? or is she/he acted upon? How does this relate to the overall theme?

Questions to Ask: Theme

Theme is the author's overall statement about the human condition. The interplay of a work's structural elements and stylistic maneuvers reveals the author's theme.

☆ What kind of characters are in the work? What kind of life, action, events are they involved in?

☆ What motivates the characters or controls their actions?

☆ What role does fate or coincidence play in the characters' fortunes?

☆ From what point of view is the story told? Does its scope have any bearing on the overall theme?

☆ What unusual structural devices or stylistic techniques does the author use? How are they related to the theme?

☆ Are there recurring images—symbols—in the work? How do they relate to the theme?

Chapter Checklist

Chapter _____   **Page** _____ **through Page** _____

Summarize the action/plot development:

What characters are introduced?

Does the action/plot development clarify or resolve questions raised in previous chapters? If so, how?

What role does setting play? Does it have any effect on the characters or plot development?

Is there any change in narrator or point of view? If so, what is the effect?

Does the personality of any of the characters change? If so, why?

Does the chapter end with a "cliff-hanger," or is it a self-contained unit? What is the significance of this?

What is the "pace" of this chapter? How is this achieved?

What is the overall function of the chapter within the entire work?

What is the thematic function of the chapter in relation to the plot development?

What is the emotional tone of the chapter? How is this achieved?

Pages to Remember:

Comments:

Book Report Worksheet

Title: _____

Author: _____

Footnote Entry:

  for a book or play

_____, _____
          (author)   (title)

(_____ : _____, _____), p. _____.
     (location)   (publisher)   (date)   (page)

  for a short story or poem

_____, " _____ ", _____
        (author)   (title)   (work it is

_____, ed. _____ (_____ :
contained in)   (editor/author)   (location)

_____, _____), p. _____.
     (publisher)   (date)   (page)

Book Report Subject: _____

Book Report Topic: _____

My focus: _____

My approach: _____

My emphasis: _____

Genre: _____ Type: _____

Number of Chapters: _____ Acts: _____ Stanzas: _____

Time of Events: _____

Location of Events: _____

Major Characters (Give full name, nickname, occupation, age, relation):

Minor Characters:

Give a brief summary of the plot/action of the work:

Give a brief summary of the subplot(s). Explain the function/effect of the sub-
   plot(s) on the main plot/action of the work:

Identify the narrator and the point of view. Explain the impact of these on the
   plot/action:

Identify the author's main methods of characterization:

Describe the balance between the author's use of description and narration:

Identify the author's characteristic use of language:

Describe the time scheme employed in the plot:

Explain the significance of the work's title:

Give a brief summary of the work's theme(s):

Comment on the author's success in presenting this theme:

Put the work into context: how does it relate to other works . . .
     by the same author?

     of the same genre and type?

     on the same subject?

     of the same style?

     of the same period?

Book Report Worksheet
Sample Book Report: *The White Album*

Title: _The White Album_

Author: _Joan Didion_

Footnote Entry:

    for a book or play

    ___Joan Didion___ , ___The White Album___
        (author)   (title)

(_New York_ : _Washington Square Press, 1979_), p. _____ .
  (location)   (publisher)   (date)   (page)

    for a short story or poem

  _____ , " _____ ", _____
      (author)   (title)   (work it is

_____ , ed. _____ (_____ :
 contained in)   (editor/author)   (location)

_____ , _____), p. _____ .
  (publisher)   (date)   (page)

Book Report Subject: _Joan Didion's The White Album—selected chapters_

Book Report Topic: _Biblical parallels—overall structure and images_

My focus: _how Didion uses parallels to reinforce her themes_

My approach: _two-track (requires some knowledge of Bible)_

My emphasis: _aesthetic – archetypal (combination)_

Genre: _nonfiction_   Type: _collection_

Number of Chapters: _20_   Acts: _____   Stanzas: _____

Time of Events: _1960s_

Location of Events: _Southern California (a few other places mentioned)_

Major Characters (Give full name, nickname, occupation, age, relation):

    — not related to conventional "plot" — individual chapters on "newsmakers" and "stars" of 1960s — Eldridge Cleaver, Jim Morrison, Bishop James Pike, Doris Lessing, etc.

Minor Characters:

    — more of above, mentioned briefly: Janis Joplin, Peter Fonda, Nancy Reagan, etc.

Give a brief summary of the plot/action of the work:

    —Didion collected sketches and essays she had written about her observations and responses to a variety of people, places, events — all seem to be part of or symbolic of the turmoil of the 1960s.

Give a brief summary of the subplot(s). Explain the function/effect of the sub-
   plot(s) on the main plot/action of the work:

— a few chapters focus on personal events in
Didion's life — e.g. a trip to an orchid greenhouse —
seem to be instances of personal confusion
reflecting the larger chaos.

Identify the narrator and the point of view. Explain the impact of these on the
   plot/action:

— first person: in most chapters Didion is both
participant and observer; in others, the subject, too.
Reinforces the theme of being trapped in a crazy world.

Identify the author's main methods of characterization:

— Didion is an objective reporter sometimes,
a commentator at other times — if she's witnessing
something, she lets the subjects do the talking
and acting.

Describe the balance between the author's use of description and narration:

— when it involves people, it depends on whether
she's directly involved (see above) — with places
and events (e.g. Hoover Dam), she narrates her
own thoughts.

Identify the author's characteristic use of language:

— a blend of deadpan, "hip" sarcasm, Biblical
images — frequently interrupted by her direct
voice.

Describe the time scheme employed in the plot:

— centers on the 1960s.

Explain the significance of the work's title:

— could be any number of things — the psychiatrist's
report, her notebooks.

Give a brief summary of the work's theme(s):

— everything is falling apart — everyone is out for selfish gratification with no responsibility for effects of personal behavior — people are deluded by fantasies and "isms" — violence is rampant.

Comment on the author's success in presenting this theme:

— Didion's jumbling of topics and "types" creates shocking images — her deadpan, understated description of horrible events reinforces her points on numbness, chaos, imminent destruction.

Put the work into context: how does it relate to other works . . .

by the same author? *read Slouching Towards Bethlehem, another of her collected essays about that generation — same horrified tone, same bizarre subjects and observations.*

of the same genre and type?

—

on the same subject?

—

of the same style?

—

of the same period?

—

Chapter 9

Sample Book Reports

**Catching on to *Catch-22*
The Book of Joan: Joan Didion's *The White Album***

SAMPLE BOOK REPORTS

Catching on to *Catch-22*

For a student of literature like me, raised on straightforward fiction like *Wuthering Heights* and *The Jungle*, my first venture into Joseph Heller's *Catch-22* seemed doomed. I felt the plot was leading me around in a maze. I wondered why the author would introduce a subject and then shy away from it, only to return to it unexpectedly, maybe repeatedly. From the few literary allusions that I managed to recognize, like his parody of Tennyson . . .

> . . . in the spring Milo Minderbinder's fancy had turned to thoughts of tangerines[1]

. . . I inferred that I was missing many more allusions that must be vital for total comprehension.

What kept me reading, then? Why do I now want to reread *Catch-22*?

I was led through the maze mainly by the humor. As I moved step by step through the difficult terrain, I was tempted further with irreverent gags promising shocking revelations and ever more gags. "Nately had a bad start. He came from a good family" (p. 12). Dunbar was "One of the finest, least dedicated of men" (p. 14). "All over the world, boys . . . were laying down their lives for what they had been told was their country" (p. 16). I soon discovered that Heller's purpose is to make the reader laugh so that he will not weep, so that he can survive Heller's savage attacks on one social condition after another: the white man's persecution of the Indian, the greed of some M.D.s, the tyranny of life in the armed forces.

Most of these conditions are summed up in Heller's original phrase, "Catch-22." That is, the powers that be will plant a hidden trick in every situation. For example, the battle-weary men of the 256th Squadron, assigned to bomb the Nazis in Italy and France, are promised that when any flier completes thirty-five missions, he will be rotated back to noncombat duty. But whenever Captain Yossarian, the main character, and his fellow Air Corps men near that goal, their colonels raise that number: to forty, then to forty-five, soon to sixty-five! The colonels want to build up the best record of any squadron. That's easier with veterans like Dunbar, Nately, and Yossarian than with the green recruits who would replace them in rotation.

Likely to die then not for his country but for his colonels, Yossarian finds all avenues of appeal blocked by those same commanders. He tries to escape first by feigning illness, then insanity. "Doc" Daneeka agrees he would have to ground any airman who is proved insane. But there's a catch. The airman must ask to be grounded. Anyone who wants to be relieved of combat duty thereby proves he is not crazy. And if he's proved sane he must go on flying.

Once I understood that official deception is the main theme, I began to see the

[1]Joseph Heller, *Catch-22* (New York: Simon and Schuster, 1961), p. 246. All further page references will be made in the text.

unity of Heller's encyclopedic subject matter. To Heller, the government, Big Business, and all the professions are evil. The only real heroism left is the courage to refuse to conform. Three characters—Orr, the Chaplain, and Yossarian—decide that the only way to become virtuous is to disobey the Evil Establishment.

The way Heller develops his characters, at first very puzzling to me, proved to be true to Yossarian's psychology. Whenever he recalls the death of Sergeant Snowden in the bombing of Avignon, Yossarian can remember only certain details before he shies away from the full memory. But each of the eight times that he thinks of Snowden, he manages to recall more. Finally, at the crisis of the novel, delirious over an "odious deal" he has made with the colonels, he gains the strength to think through the entire Snowden situation. With that strength, he renounces the deal and he deserts.

Heller's plot, then, is not really a maze; it's a deliberate circling eight times around a traumatic memory, coming closer each time to the central agony.

Heller uses another method of story telling that has taken me longer to appreciate, and it's one of several reasons that I must reread *Catch-22*. (Others: to experience again the vivid descriptions of aerial maneuvers and to resavor the great one-liners.) This method, I have learned by consulting a book on how to analyze fiction[2], is called the archetypal approach. I was alerted to the fact that Heller uses it when Yossarian, perched naked in a chestnut tree, tells the black marketeer, Milo, that the tree is really the Tree of the Knowledge of Good and Evil. I put this together with the way the Chaplain sees the scene from a distance: A naked man in a tree is offered something to eat by a man in dark clothing. The Chaplain does not translate this into words, but we are able to do so for ourselves: Yossarian is Adam, Milo is Satan.

I have learned to look for "second meanings," to realize, for example, that Heller wants his reader to feel an emotional relationship between Yossarian's situation and Adam's. I expect, then, that if I reread *Catch-22* with greater attention to allusions and archetypes, I will find whole new dimensions of theme, plot, and character to appreciate.

[2]Walter James Miller and Elizabeth Morse-Cluley, *How to Write Book Reports* (New York: Arco Publishing, 1984), pp. 12–13.

The Book of Joan: Joan Didion's
The White Album

It is a lonely, crowded world described in Joan Didion's *The White Album*, a collection of essays and profiles chronicling the 1960s in Southern California. And no one is lonelier than its author-narrator, who is almost paralyzed by what she observes. She is compelled to apologize for even recording what she observes! "I want to tell you this not as aimless revelation," she pleads at one point, "but because I want you to know, as you read me, precisely who I am and where I am and what is on my mind."[1]

She is a modern-day Jonah, running away to Hawaii or orchid-filled greenhouses trying to escape what she sees, but driven by her creative gift to

[1]Joan Didion, *The White Album* (New York: Washington Square Press, 1979), p. 134. All further references in this paper will be made to this edition of *The White Album*.

record the apocalyptic Sixties, to chart the social and psychological disintegration of a generation. In the first chapter of the book, she tries to justify her need to make sense of the senseless. "We live entirely, especially if we are writers, by the imposition of a narrative line upon disparate images" (p. 11).

Some readers might find Didion's sequence and choice of topics random and decide that no relationship exists between any of them except for the decade they cover. Yet, not only does this choice reflect the explosive, psychedelic randomness of the 1960s, but it also indicates Didion's conscious decision to mimic the structures and images of the Old Testament as a means of reinforcing her themes.

The books of the Old Testament have no conventional "plot." Yet the characters, setting, and themes are perfectly clear. As a whole, the Old Testament is a chronicle filled with high drama, prophets and philistines, tales of floods and desert exiles. Joan Didion's *The White Album* is a modern anti-epic history of comparable structure and style.

The language she uses to describe the setting of Southern California conjures up the arid and plague-ridden world of the ancient Middle East. The oppressive heat, the constant threat of earthquakes, droughts, brushfires, rattlesnakes, scorpions—her vivid, hellish descriptions could be applied to any of the doomed kingdoms in the Old Testament.

And the psychological atmosphere she records is a chilling echo of a society ripe for the wrath of an angry Jehovah. In her characterizations of the modern-day Pharisees and Philistines, Didion makes her most shocking parallels. She exposes the vacuous values of the Hollywood "stars"—their phony liberalism and solidarity with the oppressed—as publicity-seeking "events" designed to manipulate the very people they pretend to champion.

In a land where charity is so cheapened, it is no surprise to see the trivial raised to the solemn. Didion takes the two main features of the Southern Californian terrain — the highways and the coast — and presents damning sketches of the people who run them. In their isolated computer rooms, the people regulating traffic flow are like pharaohs, pushing buttons, watching remote screens, conducting experiments on the hapless hordes of motorists far away. In Malibu, middle-aged lifeguards glorify their endless summers with military drills and the jargon of centurions.

Even the architecture Didion chooses to mention evokes Biblical echoes. The governor's palace/estate built by Ronald Reagan—and shunned by the hermit-like Jerry Brown—is a vulgar monument to ego and conspicuous consumption, a modern-day Tower of Babel. The Hoover Dam hums and looms like a hydraulic Goliath, and shopping malls "float on the landscape like pyramids" (p. 179).

Few Biblical prophets were considered sane. And Didion in real life was diagnosed as a paranoid. But she was not the only voice crying out in the cultural and spiritual desert of the 1960s, as three of her personality sketches show.

Didion's chapter on J. Paul Getty's museum presents an oddly sympathetic portrait of the millionaire and a scathing condemnation of the museum tourists. The museum's relentless opulence makes them uneasy. It is a strange reminder that greed—and the greedy—have always existed, that the antique wealth they buy for their homes now were the tacky trinkets of the idle rich centuries ago. The absent, eccentric builder, J. Paul Getty, looms like a dour Isaiah throughout the chapter.

Getty's mute message is countered by the shrill, imperious warnings of our modern Jeremiah, Doris Lessing. She is, as Didion describes her, a woman who "writes exclusively in the service of immediate cosmic reform" (p. 120). Although a flashier visionary than Didion, Lessing too is disheartened by the chaos around her and suffers "doubts not only about what to tell but about the validity of telling it at all" (p. 125).

The final member of this unlikely trinity in the unholy land is the clear-sighted seer, Georgia O'Keefe, who rejects the hype and hypocrisy and retreats to the purity of the desert and her art. A model of introspection and integrity, she is as much John the Baptist as she is Ruth.

But for every Ruth there is a Salome, for every prophet there is a philistine or zealot. And in *The White Album*, Didion provides the foils in this archetypal balancing act. There is Bishop James Pike, the opportunist whose messianic arrogance ends in the desert heat. There is the fundamentalist preacher, Brother Theobald, a pop-hip version of Moses, leading his flock to Tennessee to await the Apocalypse, "participat[ing] in the national anxieties only through a glass darkly" (p. 98). Equally misled are reactionary Jaycees bemoaning the loss of the good old days, and the feminists, their holy war sinking in a swamp of paradoxes.

And no Biblical parallel would be complete without satanic demons and anarchic idols. *The White Album* completes the psychological landscape with Charles Manson, Janis Joplin, Peter Fonda and the biker movie cult, Eldridge Cleaver and Huey Newton, and Jim Morrison of The Doors, the "missionaries of apocalyptic sex" (p. 21).

Any writer who tries to capture the temper of a historical period runs the risk of giving a lopsided view. But few periods in history have resembled the 1960s, a time when every institution, every belief, every facet of life was undergoing violent transformation. Didion could have chosen any number of personalities to serve as models, any number of incidents or monuments to serve as symbols. But because she chose those people, incidents, and monuments with which she had personal contact, she reinforced the central theme of her book and the tragic lessons of the 1960s—the pursuit of personal freedom brings social anarchy, the pursuit of individual pleasure brings collective pain.

No one writing from the safety of distance or time can capture the reality of a world self-destructing. Didion's painful self-awareness amidst the hypocrisy and hedonism and her inspired metaphor of the Biblical Old Testament produce a modern testament to the power of art. And, as such, *The White Album* stands as proof that literary nonfiction has come of age.

Whether you are writing an authoritative report on a novel or a naive report on a collection of poems, you will find our appendix and two indexes very helpful.

In the appendix, Master List of Critical Concepts for Book Report Writers, we have listed the major concepts and facts you might need to know to understand a particular genre or literary style. Some words appear in more than one list—*plot* or *setting*, for instance—since you would need to understand the elements of plot for both fiction and drama, or the significance of setting in both nonfiction and fiction.

You will find these major concepts and facts listed alphabetically in the Subject Index with their specific page references.

The second index, the Author and Title Index, lists all proper names and titles of the many literary works and writers, psychologists, and scientists discussed in this book.

Master List of Critical Concepts for Book Report Writers

Analyzing and Evaluating Literature

aesthetic emphasis
approach, book report
archetypal emphasis
archetypes
authoritative approach
"collective unconscious"
context, literary
critical conclusions
"depth psychology"
emphasis, book report
focus, book report
"free association"
function of literature
id, ego, and superego
ideological emphasis
"identity crisis"
myth(-opoeia)
naive approach
patterns in literature
psychological emphasis
sociological emphasis
subject, book report
topic, book report
two-track approach
universal themes in literature
vicarious experience in literature

Writing the Book Report

bibliography
brackets, use of
critical conclusions
definition
description
editing quotations
ellipsis, use of
footnotes and endnotes
internal reference
introductions
italics, use of
paraphrasing quotations
plagiarism
quotations, direct
quotations, indirect

Literary Styles

Age of Reason
Anglo-Saxon (Old English) poetry
Classicism
Expressionism
formal style in nonfiction
Impressionism
informal style in nonfiction
Naturalism
Neoclassicism

"New Journalism"
plot structure, nontraditional
plot structure, traditional
Realism
Romanticism
"total theater"

Analyzing and Evaluating Fiction

antagonist
anti-hero
archetype
characterization
climax
confidante
conflict, inner and outer
description
dialogue
disequilibrium
exposition
foil
internal monologue
irony, dramatic
irony, verbal
main character
mood
motif
motivation
narration
narrator
plot
point of view
protagonist
round and flat characters
scene
setting
short story
summary
suspense
symbol(-ism)
sympathetic and unsympathetic characters
theme
tone
type character
universal themes in literature
verisimilitude
vicarious experience in literature
walk-on character

Analyzing and Evaluating Drama and Plot

"Absurdist" drama
allegory
antagonist
anti-hero
archetype
"bitter comedies"

catharsis
character drama
characterization
climax
comedy
complication
confidante
conflict, inner and outer
denouement
dialogue
disequilibrium
drama, formative elements of
dramatic reversal
exposition
foil
Freytag's Pyramid
hamartia
in medias res
initial moment
irony, dramatic
irony, verbal
language, dramatic
main character
mood
motif
motivation
narration
plot
props in drama
protagonist
radio drama
round and flat characters
setting
situation drama
"Slice of Life" drama
sound effects in drama
spectacle in drama
stage directions, role of
stichomythy
suspense
symbol(-ism)
sympathetic and unsympathetic characters
tableau(x)
theme
tone
"total theater"
tragedy
tragic flaw
tragic hero
tragicomedy
type character
universal themes in literature
verisimilitude
vicarious experience in literature
walk-on character

Analyzing and Evaluating Poetry and Language

allegory
alliteration
allusion
Anglo-Saxon (Old English) poetry

assonance
ballad stanza
blank verse
caesura
collections
couplet
description
dialogue
diction
dissonance
end-stopped line
English sonnet
exposition
figures of speech
fixed meter
foot, metric
free verse
full rhyme
half-rhyme
heroic couplet
irony, verbal
Italian sonnet
language, dramatic
loose meter
metaphor
mood
"music," language as
onomatopoeia
ottava rima
paradox
prosody
puns
quatrain
rhythm in poetry
rime royal
run-on line
Shakespearean sonnet
sonnet
Spenserian stanza
"sprung rhythm"
stanza
stichomythy
stress patterns in poetry
strophe
symbol(-ism)
syntax
theme
tonal patterns in poetry
tone
universal themes in literature

Analyzing and Evaluating Nonfiction

allusion
analysis
anecdote
argumentative nonfiction
autobiography
biography
characterization
collections
critical conclusions
definition

description
example
exposition
expository nonfiction
figures of speech
formal style in nonfiction
historical narrative
informal style in nonfiction
introductions
memoir
mood

motif
narration
narrator
"New Journalism"
point of view
scene
setting
speculative nonfiction
summary
suspense
theme
tone

Subject Index

Author and Title Index